Where Road Ends

Havasu Palms...
Recipes & Remembrances

Compiled & Written by
Bobbi Ann Johnson Holmes

Robeth Publishing
Lake Havasu City, Arizona USA

Copyright © 1995 by Bobbi Ann Johnson Holmes
All rights reserved including the right of
reproduction in whole or in part in any form.

This book was published and produced exclusively by Robeth Publishing and was not affiliated with or sponsored by Havasu Palms, Inc.

Robeth Publishing
Post Office Box 223 Lake Havasu City Arizona, 86405

Cover photographer Terri Blanker.
Historical photographs courtesy Caroline Johnson. Although many of the original photographers are unknown, we would like to thank them for preserving a moment in history.
Photographs circa 1995, Photographer Bobbi Holmes.
A special thanks to my editor, Caroline G. Johnson.
Thanks to Valdis Avots, Lake Havasu Camera, for photo reproductions, to Alan Teeple, Donaldson's Instant Printing, for photo screening and to Dean Rowe, for editing consultation.
Information for portions of the local history from oral history interviews. To the best of our knowledge no false information has been intentionally included.
Recipes generously donated by tenants, employees and other friends of Havasu Palms, Inc.
Manufactured in the USA by Morris Publishing, Kearney, Nebraska
Library of Congress Number 95-72879
ISBN 0-9649956-0-3

Dedicated to my parents,

Walt & Caroline Johnson

"We got sewers overflowing and
the bathrooms need cleaning,
trash gets emptied just twice a week.
Walt's fixin' water pipes as fast as he can.
Gotta make a livin' he's a Havasu man.

"Caroline's washing clothes
and yelling at Mike.
Always tellin' people little Fritzie won't bite.
Walt takes off and he's flyin' away,
Caroline says it's a wonder I'm not gettin' grey.

"We got some trailer pads,
but we need more.
Tryin' to get them in is strictly a bore.
Indians raisin' heck about a shack in the back.
If I ever leave here I'm not comin' back.

"They got a little girl,
her name is Bobbi Ann.
She catches the eye of every young man.
She works in the store all during the day,
and then she says Daddy can I have my pay.

"Here stands Tim, a quiet spoken guy.
When he's on a water ski he surely can fly.
We got speed boats racin' in the five mile zone.
I'm sittin' here pleadin',
        oh please go home!"

Havasu Man, (1968)
by Mike Russom

Top photo: Havasu Palms Store, with a view of Pilot Rock, 1995.
Bottom photo: Havasu Palms swimming beach, 1995.

Contents

Remembrances

Before Parker Dam	7
Birth of the Havasu Man	11
From Then to Now	15
This Wilderness	19
The Airstrip	23
Via Water	25
Road's End Restaurant	30
Gallery of Photographs	39

Recipes

Appetizers & Beverages	72
Soups, Salads & Vegetables	78
Meat & Poultry	91
Main Dishes & Casseroles	96
Breads	110
Pies, Pasty & Desserts	114
Cakes, Cookies & Candy	120
Miscellaneous	131
Index	135

Order Form

137

The top photo shows Road's End Camp, 1940. Road's End Camp's first dock (bottom photo) was built by Al Sanderson and his son Glen in 1943. Later Bud Sickles added onto the dock. He rented fishing boats, charging $3 a day for a row boat and $5 a day for a motor boat - which included a tank of gas.

Before Parker Dam

Before Parker Dam was built in the 1930's, the area now known as Lake Havasu was a portion of the Colorado River, bordering the states of California and Arizona. According to A. L. Kroeber's *Handbook of the Indians of California*, the Mohave and Halchidhoma tribes made their homes along the California side of the Colorado River. The border of the two tribal territories was south of the present location of Havasu Palms. To the Halchidhoma's southern border lay the Yuma territory.

The Mohave Indians chased the Halchidhoma from the area, and eventually invited various bands of Chemehuevi (who lived to the northwest of the Mohave) to live along the Colorado River. Tensions later developed between the two tribes, and the

Chemehuevi were driven from the area for a time.[1]

By 1900 the lands along the California side of the Colorado River was open to homesteading. In 1907 the Secretary of Interior anticipated that Congress would be adding lands to various Mission Indian reservations. Because of this, he withdrew land along the California side of the Colorado River from *"all forms of settlement and entry, pending action by Congress authorizing the addition of the lands described to the various Mission Indian Reservations."*[2] Although the Chemehuevi Indians were not Mission Indians, they were mentioned by Special Agent Kelsey, who submitted the report to the Secretary of Interior, which prompted the land withdrawal.

In 1921 the Bureau of Indian Affairs processed public domain allotments along the California side of the Colorado River, under the provisions of the Allotment Act of February 28, 1891, for seven Indians. According to history professor, Stephen Beckham, of Lewis and Clark College, these allotments were made under a provision which dealt with non-reservation land, as opposed to reservation land. Therefore, Beckham contended that this, along with other facts showed that no Chemehuevi Reservation had been legally established along the California side of the Colorado River.[3]

When Parker Dam was built, portions of the shoreline along the river would eventually be covered by the new lake. Metropolitan Water Company purchased sections of the river shoreline. They paid both the Mohave and Chemehuevi Tribes

---

[1]A.L. Kroeber, *Handbook of the Indians of California* (1976), p. 595-596

[2] 1907 Letter of Secretary of Interior 974-Ind.Div.(1907) JES

[3]Declaration of Stephen Dow Beckham (October 14, 1992) p.4.

for land along the Colorado River. After the dam was completed, the purchased shoreline which had not been covered by water, was turned over to the Federal Government.

Before the dam was built, Havasu Palms was the location of a mining claim. After the dam was completed, one mine was covered by the new lake. The miner then secured a lease from the U.S. Fish and Wildlife Service for a fishing camp, which he named Road's End. Today you can still find Road's End Camp located on many maps. By the mid-sixties, Road's End was under new ownership and incorporated under the new name "Havasu Palms".

In 1964 the Chemehuevi Tribe received a second payment for the land along the Colorado River. At that time the Indian Claims Commission rendered a judgement in favor of the tribe for $996,834.81 for *"aboriginal lands including whatever interest it may have possessed in the alleged Chemehuevi Valley Indian Reservation on the west bank of the Colorado River."* [4]

In June of 1970 the Chemehuevi Tribe adopted one of its first constitutions, which enabled it to become a legally recognized tribe by the Federal Government.

In spite of the controversy over the legal creation of the Chemehuevi Indian Reservation, reservation boundaries have been on the maps for over forty years. In 1974 some 30 miles of shoreline, which had reportedly been purchased twice from the Chemehuevi Tribe, was added to the alleged Chemehuevi Reservation. This stretch of shoreline began north of Lake Havasu City, at Havasu Landing, and extended beyond the southern border of Havasu Palms.

---

[4]Declaration of Stephen Dow Beckham (October 14, 1992) p.6.

Top Photograph: Road to the original Havasu Palms Store, abt 1968.
Bottom Photograph: Walt Johnson taking down the "Tool Shack", abt 1969. The site of the present day launch ramp.

Birth of the Havasu Man

The year was 1966. The USA was involved with an unpopular war in Vietnam, the country was struggling with civil rights, and man had not yet reached the moon. In spite of a growing population of flower children, anti-war protests, and political marches, families continued to dream and move forward.

One of these was my own. My father, Walter Clint Johnson, was a general contractor. My mother, Caroline Glandon Johnson, was the traditional homemaker, seeking no career for herself outside of our family.

As an independent general contractor, Walt began specializing in commercial buildings. It proved to be a smart move, as the housing industry in Southern California declined in the late sixties. Even more fortunate, was the business relationship he forged with Winchell's Donut House, which kept him busy building one donut house after another.

In the late sixties our family took several water ski trips to Lake Havasu. We'd previously enjoyed numerous holidays at the river along the Parker Strip. Long time friends, Gene and Margaret Mushinskie suggested our family try Havasu. We camped across the bay from the Nautical Inn, at a beach where the channel now cuts to make way for the London Bridge.

My mother's eldest brother, Ken Glandon, told us of a campground, Havasu Palms, for sale along the California side of Lake Havasu. From a vehicle's prospective, Havasu Palms, California in 1966 was a world away from Lake Havasu City, Arizona. There was no highway in those days which connected the southern end of the city to the Parker Strip. Unless you traveled via water, a voyager needed to commute through Twentynine Palms and Needles California, in order to reach Lake Havasu City from Parker.

Havasu Palms, Inc., originally named Road's End Camp, is located some 12 miles north of Parker Dam, California. Today, as it was in 1966, the last eight miles of road is dirt, winding through the rugged, yet picturesque, Whipple Wash.

We discovered a quaint fishing camp, littered with unsightly shacks, a dilapidated general store, pieced together with weathered boards and planks. Rickety wooden boat slips dotted the shoreline, while an enormous array of debris - tires, old cars, engines, rusted tools, reels of wire - lined the roads of Havasu Palms, leading from the store to camp. It offered a modest trailer park with approximately 20 pads (several were occupied) and limited camping facilities.

The then owners of Havasu Palms had a lease with the Bureau of Land Management, which ran to 1984. The leasehold included over four miles of shoreline, which bordered on the alleged Chemehuevi Indian Reservation. On this neighboring piece of property a small dirt airstrip was situated.

Walt looked beyond the tool shack, which sported an array of disgusting dried up fish heads, and the lack of telephone service, no television, and the fact that the nearest town was Parker - 28 miles away. Instead he saw the incredible sunsets over clear blue water- a retreat for fishermen, water skiers and boat enthusiasts. He saw an adventure with limitless possibilities.

When first negotiating the purchase of Havasu Palms, Walt asked the Bureau of Land Management (BLM) if there was ever the possibility the lease land could be added to the neighboring Chemehuevi Indian Reservation. He'd heard stories of unhappy business leases along the river on reservation properties. The BLM assured Walt that such an occurrence was impossible, because the shoreline was located on a public reservoir, and as such could not be part of the reservation.

Accepting the verbal assurance, Walt, along with two other business partners, bought Havasu Palms in 1967. *(The lease land was added to the reservation in 1974.)*

Although Walt's accountant thought he was crazy to leave his successful construction business, Walt convinced his wife, Caroline, and two daughters, Lynn (age 17) and Bobbi (age 13), to leave the security of home for parts unknown.

Not only were Walt and Caroline the major shareholders of Havasu Palms, they would be its general managers for the next 22 years. In January of 1968 the Johnson family moved into an old trailer, installed a mobile phone in their truck, and discovered life without television, or neighbors.

The BLM assured Walt that if he hired a professional architect to develop an acceptable master plan of Havasu Palms, and if he realigned a portion of the access road into the resort, a long term lease would be forthcoming. Walt met the demands of the BLM, yet lease negations stalled, for unbeknown to Havasu Palms, the Department of Interior was making plans to transfer the lease land to the Chemehuevi Reservation.

Without a long-term lease there could be no development loan. Armed with ambition, creativity, perseverance, hard work, humor, and the assistance of family and friends, Walt became the Havasu man and captured his dream, in spite of unkept government promises and endless challenges.

"There were flowers on the wall" - The Havasu Palms Store, abt 1969.

From Then to Now

For the first three years at Havasu Palms, my parents spent *behind the scene* time attempting to negotiate with the BLM for a long term lease, in order to secure development funding. Yet, while they waited for the elusive long term lease, and continued to pour thousands of dollars into a master plan, there were day to day tasks that needed to be done. And since there was very little extra cash, those tasks fell to family - and often to friends.

Every service at Havasu Palm is supplied by the resort. The water system, sewer system, trash disposal, and road maintenance falls on Havasu Palms Management. It seemed, in those early years, *(and sometimes even now)* that water pipes needed to be repaired on a daily basis, sewer lines needed continual unclogging, and the trash was picked up by the barrel.

My sister, Lynn, and I took control of the store. We scooped water dogs, counted minnows and night crawlers, cut 25 pound blocks of ice, and in the summer took dips in the lake between customers. The first season we painted the store a dull tan and adorned its front with brightly colored "hippy flowers". Lynn removed the disgusting fish heads from the tool shack and began hauling debris from the store via a small red wagon. She had just graduated mid-term from high school, and planned to attend college in the fall.

Walt and my cousin, Rod Wilkerson, began clearing away the trail of junk along the roadside. When dad wasn't repairing antiquated tractors and trucks, he was clearing away brush for campsites, and repairing boat docks. Caroline not only shared in the office work, she cooked for the crew, and worked along side dad, clearing campsites, and doing whatever needed to be done.

In those days we had camping, and registration took place in the store. If it was a holiday weekend campers would often register from dusk until dawn. There was something exciting about sitting on the store's stone porch at 2 a.m., watching the people and making friends during the hectic Easter holidays of the late sixties and early seventies.

It was a bit terrifying for my mother, who was shy, to be placed behind the store counter and forced to deal with customers. Yet she had the help of family and old friends, like Margaret and George Wilkerson, Elmer and Aggie Cutting, Gene and Margaret Mushinskie, and new Havasu friends, like Oma and Aubrey Head, Joy and Leon Weatherhead, Charlie and Oredelia Loyd and Pearl O'Malley.

The long term lease never materialized, major funding was never a possibility, and so the original master plan was abandoned and Walt moved forward - drawing his own plans, digging his own ditches, and building his dream with his own two hands. Crucial to the developments that were made was the assistance Walt received from one Havasu Palms owner, Walt's partner and cousin-in-law, Luanne Paul King, who helped obtain private development financing through her family.

By 1973 Havasu Palms added a hundred mobile home sites. Two years later another 27 sites were developed. The new store was completed by Easter of 1978. I recall hanging wallpaper just hours before the beginning of the holiday week.

In 1981 Walt completed the Road's End Restaurant. Not only did he design and build the building, he bartended and cooked. Together with Caroline, Walt designed the menu and developed the business into one of the most popular restaurants in the Havasu area.

Walt died of congestive heart failure on December 10, 1992. Even now, as I write this in 1995, I often hear *"Walt stories"* at the bar. Although the stories are a bit exaggerated, they tell of a generous man who would tackle any task - he was an inventor, problem solver, builder, master chef and bartender, and had one hell of a sense of humor.

When the leasehold was turned over to the Tribe in 1974, Havasu Palms was promised a long term lease if they didn't contest the land transfer. Yet a new lease wasn't secured until 1984 - and that was for a 10 year lease with a five year option. Since being placed on *"the reservation"*, Havasu Palms and its tenants no longer have all of their Constitutional rights, and must abide by the dictates of the Chemehuevi Tribe, without the benefit of any representation.

As I write this, the lease term is about to come to an end - there is a little less than four years remaining. My husband Don and I now manage Havasu Palms. The corporation continues to negotiate with the Tribe for a new lease, yet the outcome is uncertain.

With or without a lease - our family has no regrets. It has been one hell of a ride, one hell of an adventure. We've met wonderful people, forged lasting relationships, *and the stories we could tell!*

The top photo, taken in the early 1970's, shows a view of the original Havasu Palms Store. The bottom photograph shows the interior of the same building, 1968. In the early days of the "rustic" store it was prudent to inspect any garments before trying on - as scorpions were especially fond of the straw hats!

This Wilderness

Some forty years before the Johnsons moved to Havasu Palms, Caroline Johnson's parents, George and Hilda Glandon, set out with horse and buggy to their homestead in Montana. Four decades later, Hilda would liken her daughter's experiences at Havasu Palms to her own in Montana. And in many ways Caroline felt like a frontier women in this new wilderness.

Leaving behind her modern and spacious home in Covina Hills, California, Caroline's new domicile was a 10' wide trailer. The only room which would accommodate their king sized bed was the living room. By their first Christmas in Havasu, Walt had built a living room onto the trailer and placed the king size bed in the trailer living room - which was in the same room as the trailer's kitchen. Family and friends often lounged on the bed as they visited with whoever was cooking or cleaning in the kitchen.

The trailer, a 1950's vintage - was decorated in the colors of that era - which included a pink refrigerator, pink porcelain sinks, pink bathroom fixtures and pink and grey counter tops and wallboard. Caroline, who disliked pink, and was fond of the "new" color for the late sixties and early 1970's, chose to ignore the pink and grey and accent her home with avocado green. She so successfully managed to block out the pink and grey in her mind's eye, that twenty five years later, when reminded of the odd color scheme of her first Havasu home, she declared sincerely *"I would never would have done that! The fixtures weren't pink!"* It was not until she was shown a photograph that she realize it was true.

Adjacent to the trailer *(the current location of the Road's End*

Restaurant) was an oblong wood framed building. It was an obsolete motel, a series of six rooms which faced the lake. Each room had its own exit door and each room connected to its adjacent room by way of an interior door.

It was in the first room where Walt would install the family's washer and dryer. There would never be hot water in this room, but they did have electricity and running water. *"Primitive and rustic"* does not adequately describe the condition of this building. While cleaning the room, Caroline and Mike Russom killed over twenty-five black widows - they eventually stopped counting.

When moving to Havasu Palms, Walt was told they would never be able to pick up television reception. This was the era before VCR's and satellite dishes. After months without television, Walt found an antenna which picked up three stations - they were static-y, but they were better than nothing. Eventually, as Havasu City grew, television reception improved and more channels were added. Today, with satellite dishes, there are no limitations on reception.

The telephone took much longer than the TV. With no phone lines, Havasu Palms installed a mobile phone. The predecessor to the cellular, the mobile unit was not only unreliable, it completely lacked privacy. It seemed as if every mobile unit in the Parker area shared the same party line. In order to place a call, one had to listen in to the party line, then grab the free line as soon as the other party hung up. As the mobile home park expanded and no phones were available, tenants were continually borrowing the phone or making late night phone calls, requesting messages being delivered within the park.

By the 1980's Havasu Palms purchased its own phone

system. Although it only provided the park with one phone line, and there were still no pay phones for tenants, the problem of party lines was eliminated and privacy was restored.

It wasn't until 1990 that real phone service came to the park. Walt, with the help of tenants and friends, dug the trenches for the phone lines and Contel installed a microwave dish. At last, Havasu Palms had moved into the 20th century. And it was about time, for the 21st Century was just around the corner.

Aside from the technological conveniences of telephones, televisions and hot running water, Havasu Palms had to contend with its own trash collection and disposal, build sewer ponds to accommodate the growing mobile home park, keep the water system running, and maintain the only access road.

North of the community of Parker Dam California, the road winds upward several miles, leading to another small community. From there the road leads to Black Meadows and Havasu Palms. For many years much of this road was unpaved. Today the last eight miles remains unpaved - the road into Havasu Palms.

When storms wash out this section of road, Havasu Palms sends its road grader to repair the damage. Early in 1993 a portion of the road became a river for several months.

For years, metal trash barrels with plastic liners, were scattered throughout the park for trash collection. Each week, a Havasu Palms truck, pulling a flatbed trailer, would drive though camp. Those lucky enough to be on trash detail would pull the plastic bag from the barrel and load it atop the trailer for disposal in the Havasu Palms dump. That was of course - if the plastic liner had not broken. After a time it seemed easier to load the entire barrel on the trailer, returning it after its contents were disposed.

Walt grew weary of this task. Although he could not afford to purchase an automated trash truck, he was determined to build his own. A bit like Frankenstein built his monster - Walt designed and built his own trash truck, recycling parts and relying on ingenuity. Eventually the barrels were replaced by bins , and trash pickup became automated. Years later Walt purchased a used trash truck, and utilizing the knowledged acquired by building the first truck, he redesigned the second one to allow it to be run by a single operator.

Sometime after the second trash truck was put to work, the plumbing in a tenant's trailer backed up, destroying their carpet. Seeking to blame Havasu Palms, the Health Department was called to investigate. While the park was held blameless for the plumbing mishap, the inspector was fascinated with Walt's automated trash truck. He urged him to enter an upcoming contest for trash truck design - *who would have thought there were contests for such things?* Walt didn't enter, but his ugly yet efficient trash truck held a special place in his heart.

Through the years Havasu Palms continued to rely on ingenuity, creative thinking and hard work. The same as other frontier families in the wilderness.

The Airstrip

Havasu Palms' 2300' dirt airstrip was built around 1945 by Bob Orchard and his son-in law Glen Sanderson. Located on a portion of land *(adjacent to Havasu Palms' original leasehold)* on the alleged Chemehuevi Indian Reservation, tribal members were unhappy with an airstrip which they believed trespassed on their property.

Having no desire to allow its tenants or customers to continue trespassing, Havasu Palms eventually began leasing a portion of the reservation from the Tribe, which included the airstrip. The airstrip never provided income for Havasu Palms, yet it proved to be a valuable transportation alternative for tenants who disliked the primitive access road. Although this road originally traveled over the airstrip, Walt Johnson realigned it in the early 1970's.

A *land at your own risk* airstrip, most local pilots understand that all landings must begin from the lake and head to the mountains. While all take offs must be made from the mountains and head over the lake. In over 30 years the strip has been the site of only three airplane accidents.

The first occurred in the early 1970's, when a pilot decided to take off in the wrong direction - towards the mountains. The plane stalled and landed on its tail. Both pilot and passenger were cut from the plane and transported to a hospital. The outcome was never revealed to Havasu Palms. A second crash occurred with no injuries. The third crash took place during the autumn of 1995. Both pilot and passenger were seriously injured, but survived.

In the early 1970's, as Havasu Palms struggled to secure a long term lease from the BLM, Walt was forced to fall back on his previous occupation. Winchell's Donut House contracted him to build three donut houses. To enable Walt to commute to the job sites, and return to Havasu Palms for the weekends, he learned to fly.

For about a year the weekly tasks and responsibilities of Havasu Palms fell exclusively on Caroline, as Walt commuted via airplane to and from the job sites. There were no full time tenants during this period, and Caroline often found herself completely alone at Havasu Palms. Their daughter, Bobbi, was still attending high school, and she would often stay over in Lake Havasu City with friends.

One of Walt's instructors was Joe Sheble from Blythe California, who eventually became a good friend. Later - in the 1990's - a common sight at Havasu Palms' marina gas dock was the fueling of one of the sea planes owned by Joe Sheble Junior.

Via Water

Road's End Restaurant employees affectionately refer to Havasu Palms as *Gilligan's Island*. And it can certainly seem that way, when travel by land is rugged and the most common access is via water. Yet, in the early years, commuting by boat was not a practical alternative. Lake Havasu City was in its infancy - it had few businesses and no high school. Because of Parker Dam, there was no way to reach Parker by water.

Parker was where Havasu Palms first shopped. It took a long dusty hour to travel the 28 miles from Havasu Palms to Parker, Arizona. During the first half of 1968, Caroline and her daughter, Lynn, would often drive Bobbi to school in Parker Dam, then head to Parker's general store, where they would purchase candy, groceries and other dry goods for the Havasu Palms Store. When Bobbi would occasionally join one of these shopping expeditions, she felt as if she'd been transported back in time. Accustomed to the supermarkets of Southern California, she was amazed to find denims and overalls, and other dry goods being sold at the market.

When a new grocery store was built, near the current location of Lake Havasu City's Holiday Inn, Havasu Palms and its tenants began occasionally shopping by water. Yet it was not easy. Boating around the peninsula (now the island), shoppers tied up on the undeveloped shoreline and hiked up to the grocery store.

By the time Lake Havasu High School was built in 1969, Walt had grown weary of transporting his youngest daughter, Bobbi, over to Parker Dam, where she would catch the school bus to Parker. (*Lynn, who had originally driven Bobbi to school, had gone off to college and Bobbi was now in high school).* Bobbi transferred to the then new Lake Havasu High School for the beginning of her sophomore year, in 1969.

Walt assured Caroline that he would boat their daughter to and from Lake Havasu City, each weekday. *(There was not yet a paved road from Lake Havasu City to Bill Williams Bridge.).*

Many of the new students who attended Lake Havasu High School, during that first year in 1969, had attended school in Kingman. Others were new in town, as the high school offered jobs for their parents and Holly Development was busy pushing the land rush into Havasu City. (It *would not be until October of 1971 that the London Bridge would officially open).*

The first crop of Lake Havasu High School students had the unique opportunity to each begin on equal footing. Even those new to town did not have to feel like outsiders. A unique demographic factor was that students were from just about every state in the union. This helped to broaden and distinguish the student body.

After the first week of school Walt and Bobbi were boating back to the Palms. Just as they reached the 5 mile markers, at the Havasu Palms shoreline, their boat died. Within moments after the engine failed, wind suddenly kicked up and instantly churned the calm water into white caps. As Walt unsuccessfully toyed with the engine, the storm pushed their craft away from their destination, into a distant cove.

Hail began to fall, and Walt and Bobbi witnessed a small twister travel southward, along the center of the lake, heading straight for Havasu Palms. Minutes later their stalled craft was being pushed deeper into a swampy cove. As the hail plummeted down with force, Walt grabbed a life cushion, raised it over his head as a shield and yelled with glee *"Each man for himself!"*

What may have originally seemed to be a moment of despair was transformed into a humorous adventure. After the hail stopped, they secured the boat and began walking the undeveloped shoreline, heading for home. Singing marching songs and laughing, Walt and his daughter momentarily forgot their troubles.

Yet when they reached home, they discovered the roof had been ripped from their living room, and a drenched Caroline, who had not only been fraught with worry for her husband and youngest daughter, was in the mist of rescuing the contents of their living room. Fortunately, Havasu Palms tenants had pitched in (as they always have) and had come to her rescue.

Before the first month of school was completed, Walt forgot his promise to Caroline and Bobbi began driving the boat herself, thus relieving Walt of the responsibility.

For the next three years Bobbi traveled via boat to high school. At first she would moor at the Nautical Inn, yet when their docks were destroyed during a storm, she began tying up at Havasu Marina.

During that particular storm, her boat, the *Red Baron*, was washed to shore, where its hull plummeted relentlessly on the beach, causing permanent damage. From then on, Bobbi was force to bail out the boat each morning before leaving for school.

During one winter's journey from the Havasu Marina to Havasu Palms, Bobbi found herself in the middle of Thompson Bay in a boat which was rapidly taking on water. Pushing the throttle to full speed, she quickly slipped on a life jacket, and continued to move southward, keeping as close to shore as possible.

By the time she reached Pilot Rock she spotted a fishing

boat *(in those days few if any boats were on the lake during the winter)*. The *Red Baron* was close to sinking as she headed for the other boat. The unsuspecting fishermen looked up, horrified at the site of a red speed boat, driven by a deranged teenager, aiming, full speed, directly at their craft. Just before reaching the fisherman, the *Red Baron* swerved, and as it headed for the shore Bobbi yelled *"I'm sinking!"* After successfully beaching the *Red Baron*, the fishermen transported her to Havasu Palms. In spite of this mishap, she continued to boat to and from school.

Only once did Walt consider the possibility of serious harm to his youngest daughter, as a result of her boating alone. Returning from Havasu City, during the fall of her senior year, the *Red Baron* stalled in the bay outside of the Havasu Marina. Bobbi began yelling for help, but the marina was too busy to send assistance. Boaters began passing the stalled craft, yet all ignored the *Red Baron*. Time passed, and a breeze began to gain strength, slowly pushing the boat to the California side of the lake. Bobbi found herself alone on the water, moving northward, with a gale gaining force. Meanwhile Caroline had called the marina and asked if they had seen her daughter. *"She's broken down."* they said. *"And madder than hell, because no one has stopped to help her."*

Walt had already set out in search of Bobbi. As he reached the middle of Thompson Bay, within site of the Havasu Marina, there was no boat to be seen.

Moving northward, he came across floating debris - bits of scattered wood, wood which was red. Walt's face became ashen and for a moment he forgot to breathe. He continued to travel northward, praying the debris was not the remnants of the *Red Baron*. But there in the distance he spotted his daughter's red boat, fully afloat, but pushed far into a cove, partially hidden by reeds and weeds. So delighted was he to find her, he ignored the fact that she was cursing like a sailor - enraged that no one had come to help her before now.

Yet it was not always Bobbi that was being rescued. Once, while returning home during the early spring, Bobbi and a friend, Karen Witcher, were boating across Thompson Bay and Karen spotted a canoe on the far side of the lake, which had tipped over and was submerged - due to the weight of its engine. A lone man was clinging to the protruding tip of the canoe. They helped the shivering man into their boat, and after he righted the canoe, they transported him to his campsite.

As the years went on and Lake Havasu City grew, Havasu Palms began to rely more on the city across the water and less on Parker. When the Road's End Restaurant was built, Havasu Palms discovered the only practical way to obtain supplies was to transport them by supply boat. Each week the Havasu Palms pontoon boat can be seen transporting goods for the resort.

What was once a lonely winter waterway - between Havasu Palms and Havasu City - has become a well traveled highway - during all four seasons.

Road's End Restaurant as of 1995

Walt Johnson, a general contractor by trade, always knew one of the developments for Havasu Palms' future was a restaurant. Not only was a restaurant discussed in the original master plan, Walt began purchasing used restaurant equipment a good decade before construction on the building ever began. He'd also purchased, from a demolished school house site in Los Angeles, California, pallets of original red Spanish tile, which would eventually roof Road's End Restaurant.

Top Photograph: Tiling the bar floor, Road's End Restaurant, 1981.
Left to right: Lynn Galloway, Steve Galloway.
Bottom Photograph: Road's End Restaurant under construction, 1981.

Being unable to afford purchasing a California liquor license from an established business, Havasu Palms entered the California liquor license lottery and won a license in the late 1970's. Although it was good news for the resort, the pressure to build a restaurant, within the time limit set by the Department of Beverage Control was on. And since Havasu Palms was unable to secure financing *(at this time Havasu Palms was negotiating for a new lease, and the current lease was entering its last five years)*, money from cash flow and personal loans from family and friends had to be used to finance the construction.

Walt designed the restaurant's building. Yet, when he went to secure building permits from the County of San Bernardino, he was told permits were no longer required, as the location was now within the Chemehuevi Reservation. Unable to secure building permits elsewhere, Walt went ahead with construction, yet continued to adhere to local building codes. When construction was well underway, the County stepped in and announce that building permits were required. During this period of confusion over local jurisdictions *(a situation that continues today)* Havasu Palms was forced to secure extensions on the liquor license time limit. In spite of the delays and extensions, Road's End Restaurant was completed in October of 1981.

As with most Havasu Palms projects, labor came from family and friends. Peter King, the youngest son of one Havasu Palms' partner, Luanne King, worked on the construction crew. Walt's son-in-law, Steve Galloway and friend, Phillip Julien, tiled the restrooms, kitchen and floor. Don Holmes, Walt's other son-in-law, worked on tiling the roof and setting windows. Walt's daughters', Lynn and Bobbi, painted. Caroline cleaned...and cleaned. Plus, all those involved worked together assembling tables, laying carpet, and doing what needed to be done.

Top Photograph: Road's End Restaurant under construction, 1981. Left to right: Walt Johnson, Peter King, Steve Galloway. Bottom Photograph: Road's End Restaurant, October 9, 1981, the night before the grand opening. Left to right: Walt Johnson, Glen Key.

The night before the new Road's End Restaurant was to open, carpet was being laid -as Havasu Palms was scrambling to meet the final liquor license deadline. It was about 1 a.m., Walt stood, hand on hips, by the front doorway of the restaurant. He surveyed the activity - carpet was being rolled out, tables were being fastened together, and in just a few hours the Road's End Restaurant would open for business. To his youngest daughter, Bobbi, he chuckled - half serious and half in jest *"I think this is the stupidest thing I've ever done."*

In spite of Walt's declaration, he and Caroline dedicated themselves to the business. Walt's own father had owned a restaurant in Michigan, as had several of his uncles. Walt was an accomplished cook who enjoyed experimenting in the kitchen.

Before long they realized they could not purchase hamburger patties which would give them the quality they desired. Walt designed a burger press, purchased a meat grinder, and began making their own half pound burgers from choice inside round.

In spite of the disapproval from more experienced restauranteurs - those who sought bargain over quality - the Johnsons insisted on using top quality products, such as using only real butter, real sour cream, Best Food mayonnaise, preparing homemade salad dressings, homemade desserts, crisp salads and purchasing choice cuts of meat.

Caroline - who was not accustomed to commercial kitchens, which often tolerated cleaning standards far below acceptable ranges within one's home - insisted on rigid cleanliness standards, which are still in effect today. Many of Havasu Palms' repair contractors say the Road's End has the cleanest kitchen they've ever seen.

Top Photograph: Walt Johnson, using his trash truck for a "lift" while tiling the roof of the Road's End Restaurant, 1981.
Bottom Photograph: Building the walkway for the Road's End Restaurant, 1982. Left to right: Vic Sperry, Walt Johnson.

Well known for its excellent food and clean kitchen, the Road's End has also become famous for its house drink, the Road End's Cooler *(alias the Green Thing)*, which was created by Johnson son-in-law, Steve Galloway. Between 1992 and 1995, approximately 29,000 Road's End Coolers were sold.

Operating the Road's End Restaurant has not been an easy task. Most of the supplies are brought in by boat. Each week the Havasu Palms pontoon boat makes the 30 minute journey to the Lake Havasu Marina, where they meet the vendors. Supplies are then loaded onto the boat, sent back down the lake, loaded onto a truck, and driven to the restaurant. Although beer suppliers do drive the eight mile dirt road for deliveries, Havasu Palms must drive down the road to meet the liquor suppliers, who refuse to travel the rugged road.

Securing employees are another obstacle. Due to the remote location, Havasu Palms has found it necessary to house many of its employees, as daily commutes are impractical. Yet one long time Road's End employee, bar manager Terri Blanker, commutes each day via her Sea-Doo.

Since most of the restaurant customers come by boat, Road's End has developed season and non-season schedules. From mid-March through October, the restaurant is open for lunch and dinner, Thursday and Friday from 3 p.m. to 10 p.m. and Saturday and Sunday from 11 a.m. to 10 p.m. During this on-season schedule, they are also open Memorial Day and Labor Day. Road's End Restaurant closes after the last weekend in October then reopens for the off-season on Thanksgiving weekend's Friday, and remains open each weekend *(except Christmas weekend and New years Eve)* for a limited
lunch menu, through mid-March.

Much of Road's End's success can be attributed to loyal

long time employees - who remain in spite of the remote location. Gerry Guthrie, who has been with the restaurant for a decade, lives at the Havasu Palms mobile home park, as does Road's End chef, Merle Smith, who began in 1992. Head waiter and unofficial hospitality host, Gary Swint, who has been with Road's End for six years, also lives at the park.

Yet, without the continual support of Havasu Palms tenants *(who have often lent a hand as well as frequented the establishment)* and regular Lake Havasu City and Parker customers, Road's End would not have survived.

In Walt's final days, as he battled congestive heart failure, he would often sit at Road's End's "table 8" - a table normally occupied by family and off duty employees - and observe the tremendous hustle and inflow of summer customers. In a soft voice, touched with awe, he murmured, *"I never imagined it would be this successful."*

Photograph: Left to right: Steve Galloway, Walt Johnson, Lynn Galloway - the Road's End Restaurant kitchen.

37

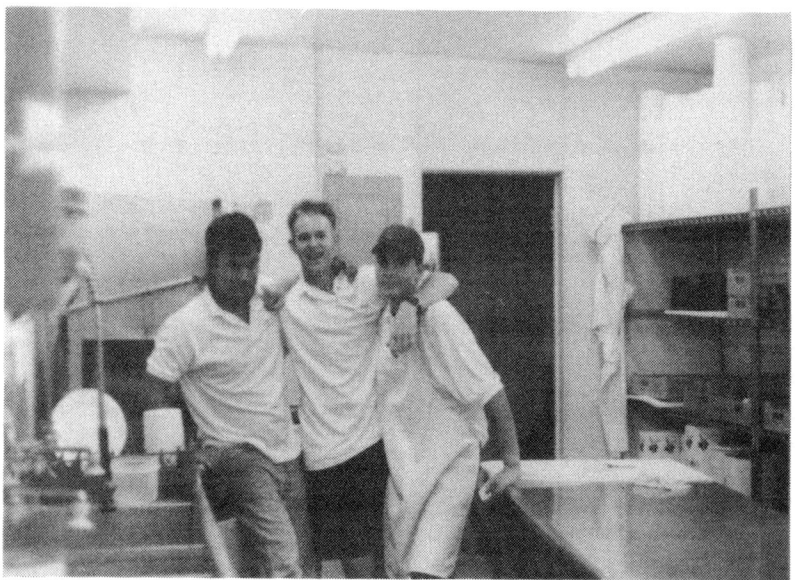

Top Photograph: The Road's End 1995 Crew. Left to right: Jeff Kelty, Terri Blanker, Phil Meeks, Gary Swint. Bottom Photograph: The Road's End Restaurant 1995 kitchen crew. Left to right: Keene Hodges, Robert Kelly, Robert "Scott" Holmes. (Camera shy: Merle Smith, Leta Marsh, Gerry Guthrie, Hoyt Jarrard, Roxanne Rengel, TC)

Gallery of Photographs

Miners Lincoln Baily and his brother came to the area before the first World War. Other early miners included the Spaniards, who worked the Kelly Gold Mine. Legend has it that the Spaniards were responsible for bringing in the original donkeys - ancestors of our wild donkeys. Local mines included: Roulette (gold mine), Islander (gold, copper and silver mine), Klondike (gold mine), Joker (gold mine) and the Lucky Lady (part of the Joker). Twenty men worked the Islander in the late 1920's.

The first known owner of Road's End Camp was J. Fleming, who leased a mine from the Baily brothers - who owned claims throughout the hills, which they frequently leased out.

Bob Orchard built the miner's shack (pictured above) in the early 1930's, before the lake was created. Today the foundation is under water.

The various owners of Road's End Camp/Havasu Palms were: (in chronological order) J. Fleming - Bob Orchard - Al and Glenn Sanderson - Bud and Kay Sickles - Homer and Pauline Willis and Noel and Mary Keefer, and their children (this group of owners changed the name to Havasu Palms) - and the most recent, Walter and Caroline Johnson, Luanne King and L .A. Moffet.

Bob Orchard built the first part of the original Road's End store about 1940. They cooked and sold hamburgers from the building and lived in a portion of the store. During this time they would also rent fishing boats.

Although it began as a joke, Bob Orchard hung a pair of pants from a flagpole to let visitors know he was home. This unusual welcome became the official "open" sign. The area pictured is the current site of the Havasu Palms Store and Marina. (Above photos taken abt 1940.)

Pictured above, the original Road's End Camp Store, about 1943. The store was rebuilt twice from Western Electric crates and other recycled material, and covered with tar paper. The store was at one end, with a beer box in the middle and a bait and storage room on the end. Gasoline, which was brought in by the barrel, was sold.

During World War II the lake was closed off and the area was used for a high artillery and gunnery range. At that time the lease was from the United States Fish and Wildlife Service. During the war the proprietor did not have to pay their lease payments, and they were only allowed to come in to protect their equipment.

The vehicles pictured are a 1940 Plymouth and a 1926 Model T, which reportedly originally belonged to Jack Kelly of the Kelly Mine.

The "Rattlesnake Hut" (top photo, 1949) was built by Mr. Fleming in the 1930's. The shack was located on Whipple Point - the current location of the Havasu Palms' travel trailer sites - in the vicinity of space 51. It earned its name because of the many rattlers that plagued the area. The shack was frequently rented out to fishermen.

The bottom photo is an early aerial snapshot of Havasu Palms.

42

The next six photographs show the shoreline along Whipple Point - the current location of the Havasu Palms Mobile Home Park. The photographs were taken in the late 1960's, when the area was used for camping. This shoreline was considered Havasu Palms' choice camping area. This section was converted to travel trailer sites in 1987.

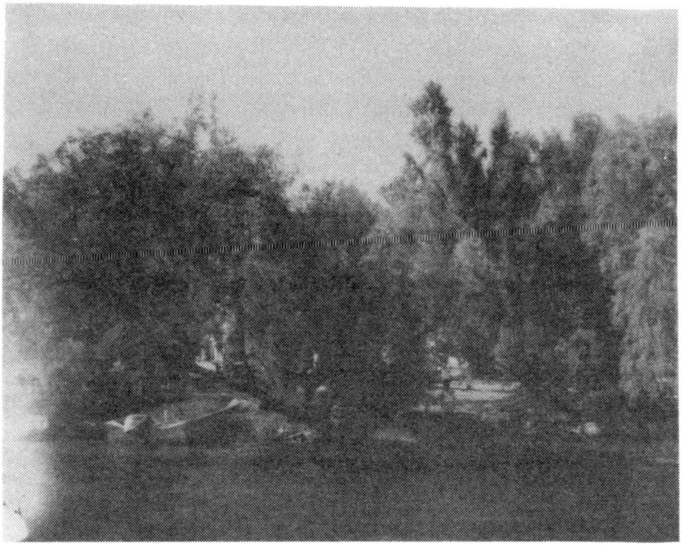

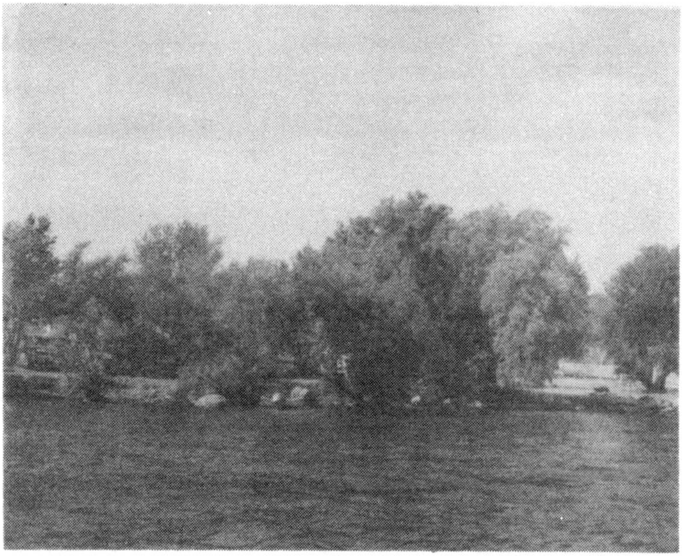

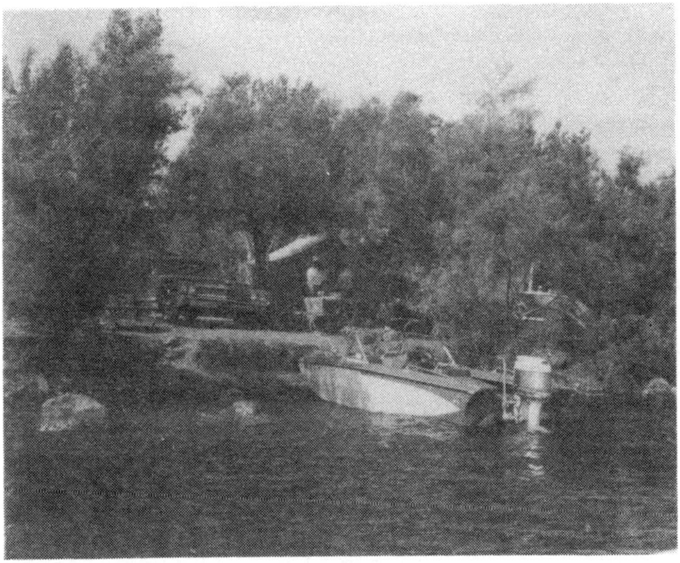

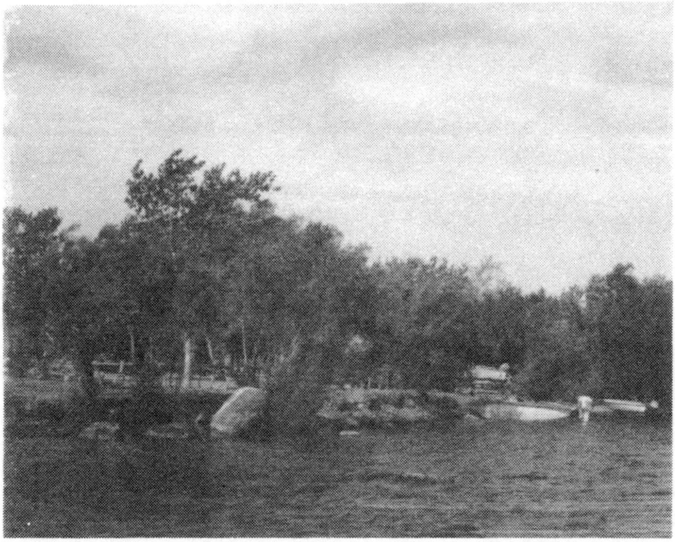

In 1968 the Johnson's left their home in the Covina Hills Ranchos, Covina, California (top photo) and moved into the "rustic" Havasu Palms trailer (bottom photo). The add-on room was built in December 1968. The trailer was located at the current location of the south end of the Road's End Restaurant. (Pictured in the bottom photo, Don Holmes and Bobbi Johnson, about 1973).

46

Top Photograph: Lynn Johnson clerking at the Havasu Palms Store, abt 1968. Bottom Photograph: Havasu Palms shack removal - demolishing an old outhouse, 1968.

During their first year at Havasu Palms, the Johnsons had house guests every weekend. Although it was a bit crowded in their small trailer, it helped ease any homesickness during the transition. Caroline Johnson had never been away from her family on her birthday, and so the family arranged a surprise party for her during their first Easter holiday. All of her siblings, their children, and her mother made it to the party. Unfortunately, their first Easter was a great deal more hectic than they had anticipated - Caroline was too busy to make it to her Birthday dinner!

Those pictured (top photo) are all April birthdays. From left to right: Penny Walker (Caroline's niece), Penny's former husband, Ken Glandon (Caroline's brother), Caroline Johnson, George Wilkerson (Caroline's brother-in-law), Aggie Cutting (close Johnson friend), and Barbara Moffet (one of the Havasu Palms owners). April 1968.

The bottom photograph is the Havasu Palms gas docks, 1968.

48

The building pictured above was situated next door to the Johnson's first Havasu Palms trailer *(at the current location of the Road's End Restaurant)*. Ordinally used as a rental motel and as a home by a previous owners of Havasu Palms, it served as Caroline Johnson's laundry room, and later as a bunk house for employees. The building was demolished in the late 1970's, to make room for the restaurant.

The bottom photograph *(taken about 1972)* shows the original stairway leading to the Johnson's first Havasu home. Rattlesnakes frequently hid along the rickety wooden stairs and in nearby rocks. The stairs were replaced with a new stairwell, which lead to the Road's End Restaurant.

In 1968 Mike Russom wrote the song *Havasu Man*, which was printed on the dedication page of this book. His verse *"Indians raisin' heck about a shack in the back..."* Is about a group of shacks that were situated on reservation land, at the border of the original Havasu Palms leasehold.

Bob Orchard and his family continued to rent this portion of land from the Chemehuevi tribe, long after he had sold his interest in Road's End Camp. They used the property for infrequent family vacations. The following four photographs show the shacks, from various views.

Orchard's permit with the tribe was on a year to year basis. By the early 1980's, the Tribe refused to renew Orchard's permit. In the early 1990's members of the Chemehuevi Tribe burned the buildings - which almost set the Road's End Restaurant afire.

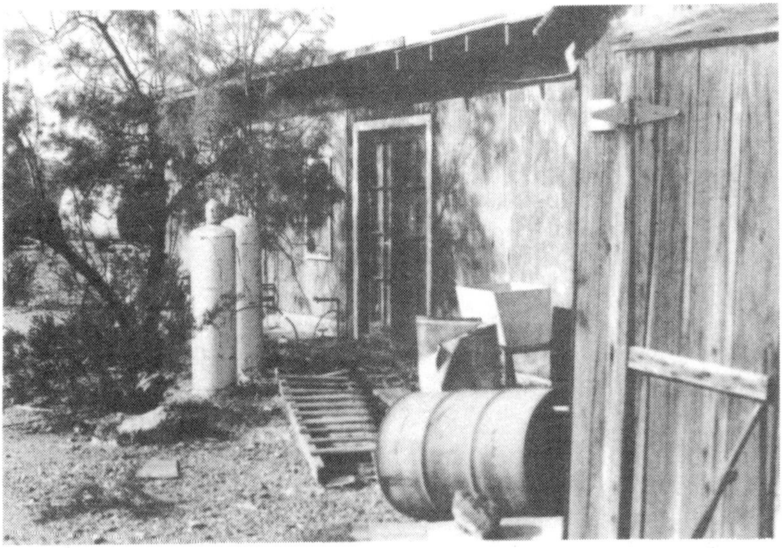

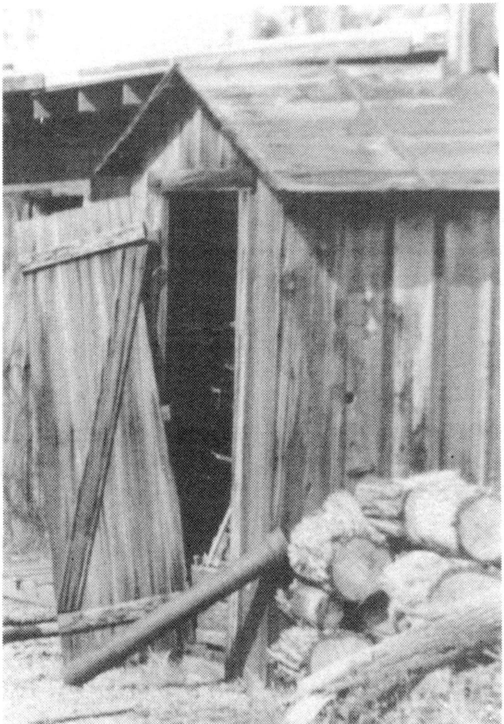

Maintenance of the dirt road into Havasu Palms has primarily fallen on the resort. In the years of *"Road's End Camp"* the road was serviced by the grader in the top photograph - it was pulled by donkeys. In later years came modern equipment. The bottom photograph shows Walt Johnson grading the road.

52

Top Photograph: Walt Johnson and Aubrey Head assemble picnic tables for the campground, 1969. Bottom Photograph (circa 1972): A barbed wire fence outlined the perimeter of the Havasu Palms lease land - separating the then Federal lease land from the alleged Chemehuevi Indian Reservation.

Before the launch ramp was moved near the Havasu Palms store, two ramps were located in the campground. The top photograph is the site of the current boat ramp. The trees were removed to make way for the launch. The bottom photo shows the area adjacent to the area pictured in the top photo. (Photos circa 1970).

54

Top Photograph: Building Walt's first trash truck, circa 1970.
Bottom Photograph: Trash detail - left to right: Mike Russom, Gary Morris, Brad Klima, Tim Loyd (driver), Hank Davidson, Chuck Loyd, and Jim Rhodes. Easter Holiday, 1972.

These two photographs show the Havasu Palms gas docks, during the late 1960's and early 1970's.

Havasu Palms' tenants have traditionally decorated a desert tree for the holidays. The environmentally conscious merry makers would always "un-decorate' the tree after the New Year. This "Christmas Tree" (top photo, circa 1970) was located on the Havasu Palms dirt road, in Whipple Wash. The decorations were usually homemade - often crafted from recyclable material.

During the 1980's a camp favorite was Havasu Palms' mascot "Number 7", pictured in the bottom photograph with Caroline Johnson. Sadly, he disappeared in 1987.

Top Photograph: Walt Johnson supervises "dynamiting" to widen the Havasu Palms dirt road. (Photo abt 1973)
Bottom Photograph: Tim Loyd and Walt Johnson remove the first Johnson Havasu home. (Photo, mid-1970's)

Flight instructor Joe Sheble, and Walt Johnson are pictured above with Walt's first airplane, a 140 Cessna, at the Havasu Palms airstrip, early 1970's. Walt Johnson is pictured in the bottom photograph, with his second airplane.

59

The one that got away. When building the new boat launch (located near the Havasu Palms Store) Walt Johnson devised a clever way to pour the concrete on land - then "launch" the ramp in place. His scheme worked too well - the new concrete ramp literally sailed out into the bay. In the top photograph Tim Loyd is pictured "retrieving" the stray ramp, and with the aid of a tractor, helped to bring it back to its final destination (about 1974).

The bottom photograph shows Walt Johnson on one of his early Havasu Palms projects - building a septic tank, 1968.

Taking a break , 1982. The top photograph shows (left to right) "Butch" George Morris, Gerry Guthrie, Lobo (Butch's dog), Walt Johnson and Charley Jones. The crew (Butch, Gerry and Walt) were taking a rest from building the courtesy boat slips to accommodate the Road's End Restaurant.

The bottom photograph shows the interior of the "new" Havasu Palms Store, built in 1978.

One of Walt Johnson's dreams for the development of Havasu Palms was the construction of modern boat slips, to replace the rickety, twenty-odd slips, which were rented by Havasu Palms' tenants.

By the winter of 1986 this project was underway - and before the spring of the same year Walt Johnson had built the new private marina - approximately 100 boat slips. Designed by Walt Johnson, the boat slips were built by Walt, Gordon Kent, Gerry Guthrie, and Jim Duckett.

The first photograph shows Walt, Gerry and "Number 7", working up at the "yard" on the slips. The second photograph shows the slips - ready for launching. The third photograph shows Walt "assembling" the boat slips in the bay. The last photograph shows the finished product.

Several years later a breakwater was added to help protect the slips from the wind. In 1991, as Walt's illness progressed, he supervised the building of street lights, which were added to the boat slips.

Unfortunately the winds and weather of Havasu create continual stress on the boat slips, and they require constant repair.

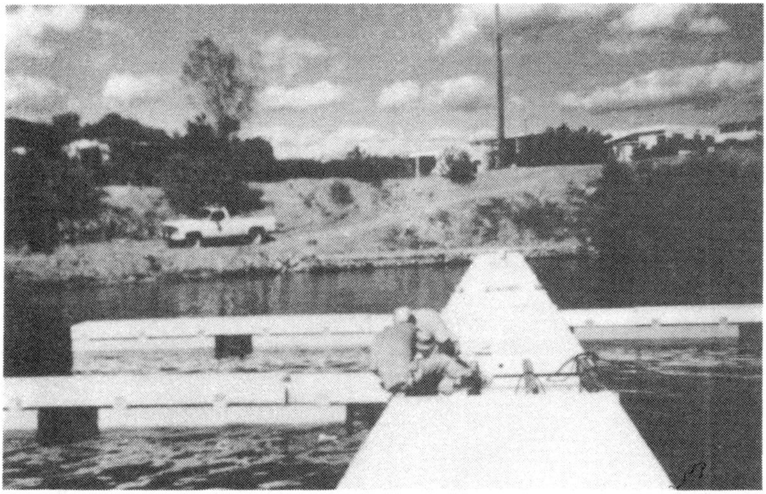

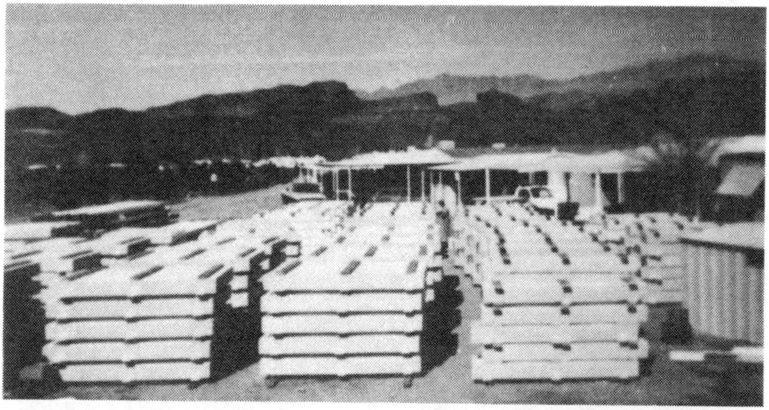

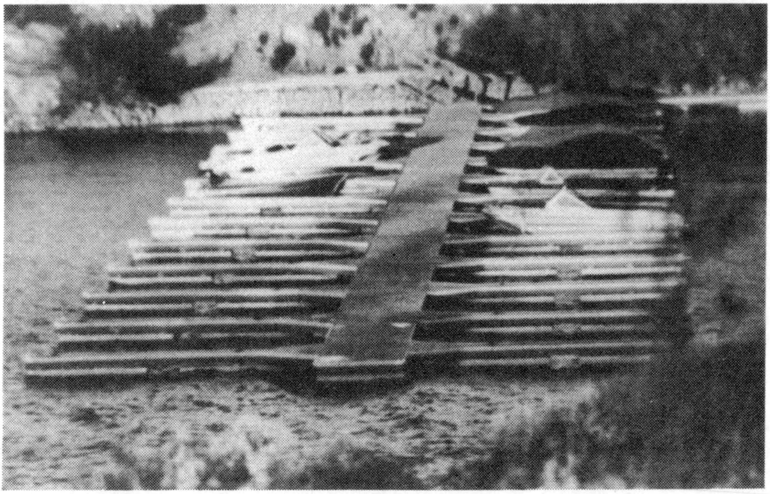

The Johnson Family - pictured in the top photograph (left to right) Elizabeth Holmes, Lynn Johnson Galloway, Margaret Wilkerson (Caroline Johnson's sister), Caroline Johnson and Bobbi Johnson Holmes. The bottom photograph was taken during the day of the christening of the Johnson's youngest grandchild, Ryan Galloway, November 4, 1990. Pictured: Walt and Caroline Johnson and their grandchildren.(Left to right): Robert Scott Holmes, Caroline Johnson, Kevin Galloway, Ryan Galloway, Elizabeth Holmes, and Walt Johnson.

64

The following four photographs show various views of the Havasu Palms Store and Marina, 1995.

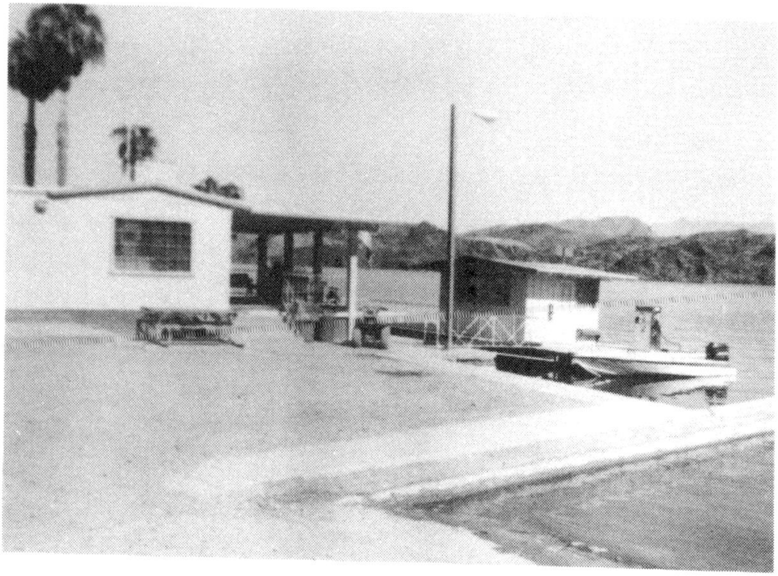

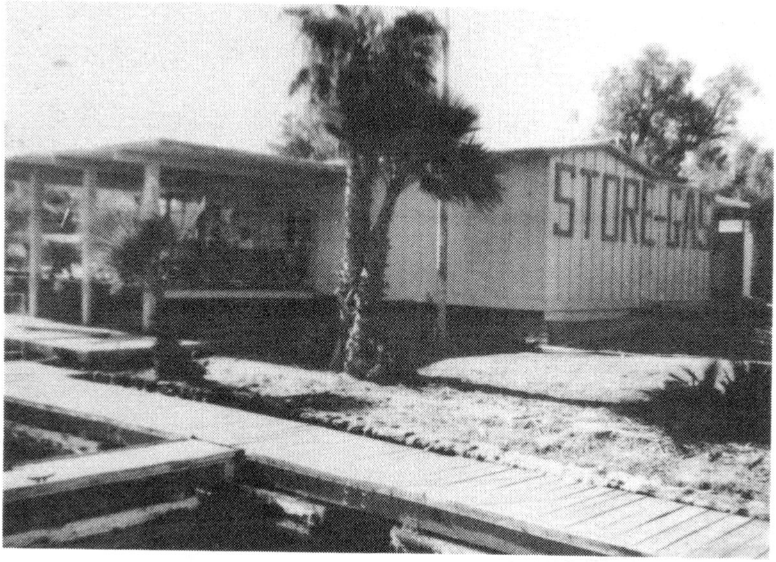
STORE-GA

Top Photograph: Don Holmes (left) and Ron Rengel (right) on the Havasu Palms Store porch - or otherwise know as "City Hall". 1995.
Bottom Photograph: Havasu Palms courtesy slips (designed by Don Holmes and Ron Rengel, in 1993). Photograph taken in 1995.

Top Photograph: By the early 1990's park models began to replace travel trailers along Whipple Bay. Havasu Palms, 1995.
Bottom Photograph: Havasu Palms Whipple Bay shoreline, 1995.

These two photographs show a view of the Havasu Palms Mobile Home Park and Marina, 1995.

The following two photographs show a view of the interior of the Havasu Palms Mobile Home Park, 1995. Cottonwood and Tamarisk trees provide shade for many of the sites.

Several years before his death, Walt Johnson built his last home, a double wide mobile home. Located at the Havasu Palms entrance, overlooking Whipple Bay, the" welcome to Havasu Palms" sign (top photo) is posted on the wrought iron fence which encloses the Johnson home.

By the end of 1993, one year after his death, Walt Johnson's memorial plaque (bottom photo) was placed as a cornerstone on the Road's End Restaurant.

The following recipes were submitted by tenants, employees and other friends of Havasu Palms. We have made every attempt to include all the entries which were sent to us. Yet, some - where obvious ingredients or directions were missing or where the writing was illegible - were not included.

When possible, recipe directions were written as submitted. All were proofed after typesetting.

Thanks to all who generously contributed to this book.

Bobbi Holmes

Appetizers & Beverages

Cheese Ball

Madeline Wilkey

1 glass jar old English cheese
1 glass jar roko bleu cheese
1 large package of cream cheese
2 shakes seasoning salt
1 shake garlic powder
1 teaspoon vinegar

Bring all cheese to room temperature. Combine and form into ball shape. Refrigerate several hours. Roll in mixture of chopped nuts and parsley. Serve with crackers.

Zucchini Fritters

Ruth Chantry

2 medium zucchini (un-peeled and sliced paper thin)
2 eggs (beaten)
1 clove minced garlic (to taste)
1/4 cup grated Parmesan cheese
1/4 cup water
1 cup flour
salt and pepper to taste

Combine ingredients, mix well. Mixture should be like pancake batter. Drop by spoonfuls into hot oil, fry until brown. Drain on paper towel.

Chicken Wings

Margaret Mushinskie

10 pounds of chicken wings
1 jar apricot/pineapple jam
1 bottle Russian dressing
1 package onion soup mix

Place clean chicken wings in large pan. Mix dressing, jam and soup and pour over chicken wings. Bake slowly at 300° for several hours.

Artichoke Dip

LaDonna Duir

14 ounce can artichoke hearts
(packed in water)
1 cup mayonnaise
1 cup Parmesan cheese
½ teaspoon garlic powder

Drain artichoke hearts and cut in pieces. Mix all ingredients. Heat for 20 minutes at 350°. Serve on crackers or with tortilla chips.

Mumm on Rye

Ruth Chantry

1 pound ground beef
1 pound Velveeta Cheese
1 pound Jimmy Dean sausage
party rounds rye bread

Saute beef and sausage in large pan. Add cubed cheese, heat until melted. Cool mixture in refrigerator for 2 hours. Spread mixture on rounds. Place on cookie sheet and broil until brown.

Beef Things

Debra Oney

2 packages sliced cooked beef
1 package cream cheese

Slice cream cheese about 1/4 inch thick, then slice again, lengthwise. Roll cheese up in beef slice. Refrigerate until ready to use. (*Taste great and they go fast. Everyone will want to know how you made them.*)

Fried Crepe Rolls

Bobbi Holmes

16 crepes
1 head shredded cabbage
1 tablespoon diced onion
1 grated carrot

1 cup cooked and diced meat
(pork, chicken or beef)
2 tablespoons butter
oil

Saute vegetables in butter. When cabbage is tender, add meat, mix and remove from heat. Spoon equal amounts onto each crepe. Fold each crepe until it resembles an egg roll. Fry in hot oil until golden brown. Drain on paper towel. Serve with hot mustard sauce.

Party Pizzas

Audrey Johnston

4 ounces tomato sauce
1 small can chopped ripe olives
2 tablespoons mayonnaise

1 small can diced green chilies
sharp chedar cheese (grated)
package French rolls

Combine tomato sauce, olives, mayonnaise, and chilies. Add cheese, enough to make a good spreading consistency. Spread mixture on sliced rounds of small french rolls. Place on cookie sheet and bake at 375° for 10 minutes.

Puttin on the Ritz

Dennis Daries

1 small package cream cheese
Ritz crackers

1 jar shrimp cocktail

Place cream cheese in center of round plate. Pour shrimp cocktail over top. Line crackers around outer edge of plate.

Snack Crackers
Lou Van Horn

2 packages oyster crackers
1 ½ cup oil
1 package Original Hidden Valley Dressing (buttermilk style)
1 tablespoon dill weed
1 teaspoon lemon pepper

Mix all ingredients (excepts crackers). Pour mixture over crackers and bake at 200° for 1 hour (stirring often) or microwave 4 to 6 minutes, stirring every minute.

Snack Crackers with Garlic
Dori Plathe

12 ounces oyster crackers
3/4 cup vegetable oil
½ teaspoon lemon pepper
½ teaspoon dill weed
1 teaspoon garlic powder
1 package Hidden Valley Ranch Dressing (original)

Mix all ingredients except crackers. Pour mixture over crackers. Keep turning until well covered. Set for 1 to 2 hours before eating. *Great for parties. Keeps for up to 2 weeks - seal well so it won't take on moisture.*

Dionysus Delight
Dennis & Susan Daries

2 sliced apples
2 sliced pears
12 ounce Gorgonzola cheese
Champagne

Slice cheese and arrange cheese and fruit on plate. Drink Champagne.

Lumpia (Filipino Egg Roll)
PJ & Bev Kramer

1 package lumpia wraps (or egg roll wraps)
2 pounds ground beef (or turkey if preferred)
5 cloves garlic (minced)
1 pound bean sprouts
2 pounds potatoes (sliced)
2 medium carrots (grated)
1 medium onion (sliced)
1 ½ pounds string beans (or frozen French cut beans)
1 can bamboo shoots (sliced)
3 stalks celery (chopped)
salt and pepper to taste

Brown onion and garlic in oil. Add ground beef and brown. Add all vegetables and spices and cook until half done. Remove mixture from heat to cool. Wrap mixture in lumpia dough and fry in enough oil to cover half of lumpia. Cook until lightly brown. *(To wrap mixture: Lay wrap flat, place approximately one tablespoon mixture across wrap, corner to corner. Fold wrap to form a triangle, fold left and right corners toward middle and fold rest of filled dough up to meet top corner to form roll. Moisten end with water to seal. Lumpia wraps are sold in oriental food stores.)* Drain on paper towel before serving.

Cocktail Meatballs

Debbie Loyd

1 pound ground beef or turkey
½ cup dry bread crumbs
1/3 cup diced onions
1/4 cup milk
1 large egg

1 tablespoon parsley
1/8 teaspoon pepper
½ teaspoon Worcestershire
1/4 cup oil
12 ounces chili sauce
10 ounces grape jelly

Mix ground meat, bread crumbs, onions, egg, milk, parsley, pepper and Worcestershire sauce. Shape into 1 inch balls, brown in hot oil in large skillet. Remove meatballs from skillet and drain off fat. In skillet heat chili sauce and jelly, until jelly is melted. Add meatballs to sauce and stir until coated. Simmer uncovered for 30 minutes. Makes approximately 5 dozen.

Oriental Style Meatballs

LaDonna Duir

Meatballs:
1 ½ pound ground beef
3/4 cup rolled oats
5 ounces water chestnuts
(drained and chopped)
½ cup milk
1/4 teaspoon salt

1 egg (beaten)
1 tablespoon soy sauce
1 teaspoon MSG
½ teaspoon onion salt
½ teaspoon garlic salt
dash hot pepper sauce

Combine ingredients and form into 1 inch balls. Brown in hot oil in large skillet. Drain off fat.

Sauce:
8 ½ ounces crushed pineapple
1 cup firmly packed brown sugar
2 tablespoons cornstarch
1/3 cup green pepper (chopped)
½ cup vinegar
(or lemon juice)
2 teaspoon soy sauce
1 cup beef bouillon

Drain pineapple, reserve juice. Mix brown sugar and cornstarch in sauce pan. Gradually stir in pineapple juice, bouillon, vinegar and soy sauce. Cook, stirring constantly, until thickened and clear. Stir in green peppers and pineapple. Add meatballs, simmer about 10 minutes for small meatballs, 5 minutes for miniature balls. Serve hot with toothpicks.

Punta Chivato Pina Coladas

Rich & Donna Middlebrough

1 cup crushed iced
½ cup whole milk
½ cup coco Lopez cream of coconut
2 pineapple rings
½ cup white rum

Blend ingredients in a blender. *Serve & slurp! The exact proportions of this drink were developed through extensive testing and sampling. This recipe is as close as we can get to the greatest pina coladas served at Punta Chivato on the Baja Peninsula.*

Havasu Hot Chocolate

Greg Tipping

3 tablespoons Carnation Hot Cocoa
10 ounces hot water
1 ounce Kahlua
½ ounce vodka
½ ounce brandy
whipped cream

Mix cocoa and water, blend. Add Kahlua, vodka and brandy. Top with whipped cream.

Soups, Salads & Vegetables

Potato Soup

Jennifer McCormick

3 cups cubed potatoes
3 green onions, sliced
2 tablespoons butter or margarine
1 teaspoon salt
½ teaspoon pepper
2 tablespoons flour
2 cups milk

Boil potatoes until soft, drain off water. Saute onions in butter. Combine four, salt and pepper, add to onions. Cook for several minutes until smooth. Add milk and potatoes to flour mixture. Cook until milk begins to boil and thickens. Season and top with cheese.

Golden Potato Soup

Mary Nichols

3 cups chopped potatoes
1 cup water
½ cup chopped celery
½ cup chopped carrots
1/4 cup chopped onions
1 teaspoon parsley flakes
dash pepper
½ teaspoon salt
1 chicken bullion cube
1 ½ cups milk
2 tablespoons flour
½ pound Velveeta cheese

Combine potatoes, water, celery, carrots, onions, parsley, seasonings and bullion. Cover, simmer 15-20 minutes or until vegetables are tender. Gradually add milk to flour, stir until well blended. Add flour mixture to hot vegetables. Cook, stirring constantly until mixture boils and thickens. Add cheese, stir until melted.

Shoe String Salad

Moe Guthrie

1 cup chopped celery
1 cup cooked chicken (or tuna)
1 can shoe string potatoes
1/4 cup chopped onion
½ to 3/4 cup mayonnaise
1 cup grated carrot

Mix ingredients well - add potatoes just before serving.

Garden Salad

Ordelia Loyd

Vegetables:
16 ounce can tiny peas (drained)
16 ounce can white corn (drained)
16 ounce can French styled green beans (drained)

1 small jar pimento (chopped)
1 cup chopped celery
½ cup chopped onion
1 cup chopped green pepper

Marinade:
1 cup sugar
½ cup oil
3/4 cup vinegar

½ teaspoon black pepper
1 teaspoon salt
1 teaspoon bean juice

Combine marinade ingredients in saucepan and bring to a boil. Cool marinade, then toss with vegetables and refrigerate overnight.

Seven Layer Salad

Dennis Daries

1 head of lettuce (chopped)
4 hard-boil eggs (chopped)
1 pound frozen peas
1 pound bacon (cooked and crumbled)

1 red onion (chopped)
½ pound Swiss cheese (grated)
1 cup Miracle Whip

Layer ingredients in bowl in order listed - beginning with lettuce and topping with Miracle Whip. Refrigerate 3 to 4 hours or overnight. Mix well prior to serving.

Broccoli Salad

Margaret Wilkerson

Salad:
1 pound bacon (fried crisp & crumbled)
4 broccoli heads (flowers only)

1 cup raisins
1 cup sunflower seeds

Dressing:
1 cup mayonnaise
1/4 cup sugar

2 tablespoons wine vinegar

Combine salad ingredients. Put dressing on salad just before you serve.

Best Macaroni Salad

Doris Castro

2 cups warm cooked macaroni
3 tablespoons oil
1 tablespoon vinegar
1 teaspoon salt
1/8 teaspoon pepper
1/3 cup pitted black olives (cut in halves)
3/4 cup diced celery
2 green onions (diced)
1/4 cup diced sweet pickle
1/4 cup diced pimento
½ cup mayonnaise

Blend macaroni with oil, vinegar, salt and pepper and toss lightly. Allow to cool thoroughly. Add remaining ingredients and mix well. Chill before serving. Makes 4 to 6 servings.

Pea Salad

Margaret Wilkerson

2 cups frozen peas
5 large mushrooms (sliced)
½ cup grated cheddar cheese
3 green onions (diced)
½ cup chopped celery
½ cup peanuts
½ cup mayonnaise
½ cup fat free sour cream

Dry peas on paper towel. Combine all ingredients and mix well.

Spaghetti Salad

Billie Bruckner

1 pound spaghetti
1 bottle Schillings Salad Supreme Seasoning Mix
1 bottle Wishbone Italian Dressing
1 ½ red onion (chopped)
2 small cucumbers (chopped)
3 tomatoes (chopped)
chopped celery (optional)
black olives (optional)
2 small bell peppers (chopped)

Break spaghetti into thirds before cooking. Cook spaghetti, drain, toss with remainder of ingredients, refrigerate.

Caesar Salad

Betty Elchuck

2 heads crisp romaine lettuce
2 cloves garlic
2 anchovy fillets (drained)
2 dashes Worcestershire sauce
juice of 2 lemons
1 egg
½ cup olive oil
salt (to taste)
fresh ground pepper
1/4 pound Parmesan cheese (grated)
croutons

Remove all wilted and torn outside leaves from the lettuce and discard. Cut the remainder of the head in half lengthwise. Wash thoroughly and shake dry. Cut into 1-1/2" wide strips and dry in a paper towel or salad spinner. Store lettuce in the refrigerator until serving time. Place the garlic, anchovy fillets, Worcestershire sauce and lemon juice in a large bowl and mash the ingredients with a fork to smooth paste. Mix the egg in with the fork, followed by the oil, salt and pepper. Just before serving, place the lettuce on top of the dressing and sprinkle with cheese and croutons. Toss the salad well to thoroughly coat the leaves with dressing. Serve immediately on large chilled salad plates.

Joy's Cabbage Salad

Joy Ward

1 head cabbage (chopped)
8 green onions (chopped)
4 ounces slivered almonds
3 ounces sesame seeds
2 packages Top Romen Noodles (crushed)
2 tablespoons butter
1/3 cup rice vinegar
1/4 cup sugar
1 teaspoon pepper
2 teaspoon salt
2 teaspoon accent
1 cup salad oil

Brown almonds and sesame seeds in butter. Cool. Combine the vinegar, sugar, pepper, salt, accent and oil, mix thoroughly. Toss all ingredients with dressing.

Chinese Cabbage Salad

Mary Waters

½ head shredded cabbage
4 green onions (chopped)
2 tablespoon sesame seeds
1 package Top Roman noodles
(uncooked and broken)
1 small package slivered almonds
½ cup salad oil
2 tablespoons sugar
1 tablespoon lemon juice

Mix together first five ingredients. In a separate bowl mix dressing from remaining three ingredients. Toss salad with dressing.

Chinese Chicken Salad

Diana Gorrell

Dressing:
1/4 cup oil
1 teaspoon salt
1 teaspoon pepper
3 tablespoons sugar
4 tablespoons rice vinegar

Salad:
1/4 cup sesame seeds
1/4 cup sliced almonds
3 chopped green onions
1 head lettuce (chopped)
1 bag Top Roman Noodles
3 skinless chicken breasts

Mix together dressing ingredients. Cook chicken, cube and cool. Break noodles (uncooked) in pieces, and toss with salad ingredient. Toss salad and dressing together when ready to serve.

Chinese Take Out Salad

Bea I. Reeg

Dressing:
1/4 cup cider vinegar
1/4 cup salad oil
2 tablespoons sugar
1 teaspoon salt
1/4 teaspoon pepper
seasoning from noodles

Salad:
1 head lettuce (chopped)
11 ounce can mandarin oranges (drained)
4½ ounces shrimp, chicken or ham (pieces)
1 package TopRoman Noodles
2 tablespoons sesame seeds
2 tablespoons margarine

Melt margarine, add noodles, stir until light tan, add sesame seeds. Toss together with salad ingredients. Combine dressing ingredients separately and toss with salad.

Hot Chicken Salad

Leta Marsh

2 cups cooked cut up chicken
1 cup diced celery
1 cup cooked rice
3/4 cup mayonnaise
1 tablespoon lemon juice
1 can water chestnuts
½ teaspoon salt
1 can creamed chicken soup
3 hard boiled eggs (chopped)
1/4 cup butter
1 cup cornflakes crumbs
½ cup sliced almonds

Mix all of the above ingredients, except butter, cornflakes and almonds. Place in greased casserole dish. Mix butter, cornflakes and almonds and top casserole. Bake at 350° for 1 hour.

(We met the Marsh family when we first moved to Havasu in 1968. Glen Marsh has worked in the Havasu Palms store for many years. Walt use to say he was the most honest employee we'd ever had. Leta, who is a sweet person and wonderful cook, worked at the Road's End Restaurant for two years.- Bobbi Holmes)

Marinated Bean Salad

Dori Plathe

Salad:
1 can yellow wax beans
1 can green beans
1 can red kidney beans
1 can garbanzo beans
1 large onion (in slivers)
½ cup red pimento
½ green pepper (chopped)
½ red pepper (chopped)

Dressing:
3/4 cup sugar
1/4 cup vegetable oil
1/4 teaspoon cayenne pepper
½ cup vinegar
½ teaspoon salt
scant teaspoon black pepper

Drain all beans and rinse kidney beans. Place salad ingredients into marinating dish. Separately, heat together the dressing ingredients. Pour over salad ingredients and store in glass jar in refrigerator.

Raw Cauliflower Salad

Debra Oney

1 head shredded lettuce
1 head shredded cauliflower
½ cup diced onion
1 pound bacon (fried and crumbled)
2 cups salad dressing
½ cup sugar
2 cups grated cheddar cheese

Mix dressing and sugar. Layer lettuce, cauliflower, onion, bacon, dressing and cheese. Cover and chill overnight. Toss before serving.

Pretzel Salad

Penny Owens

2 cups crushed pretzels
½ cup sugar
1 ½ sticks margarine
8 ounces softened cream cheese
10 ounces frozen strawberries
1 small container Cool Whip
2 cups pineapple juice
3 ounce package strawberry Jell-O
1 cup sugar

Melt margarine and combine with ½ cup sugar and pretzels. Set aside ½ cup mixture, put the remainder into a 9 x 13" *(first spray with non-stick spray)* baking dish and bake at 350° for 8 minutes. Cool. Mix together cream cheese, 1 cup sugar and Cool Whip. Spread over pretzel crust. Bring to boil pineapple juice, dissolve Jell-O and add strawberries. Let jell slightly, then place on top of cool whip layer. Top with ½ cup of reserved pretzel mixture. Refrigerate until jelled.

Hawaiian Salad

Jamie Hay

1 large can crushed pineapple (drained)
16 ounce package coconut
1 package miniature marshmallows
2 cans mandarin oranges (drained)
2 pints sour cream

Mix all ingredients together and chill. Better when done a day ahead. Garnish with maraschino cherries and mandarin oranges.

Jell-O Salad

Shirley Rojas

2 bananas (sliced)
1 cup small marshmallow
1 can chuck pineapple
2 packages small lemon Jell-O
1 egg
2 tablespoons flour
2 tablespoons butter
1 cup sour cream
2 ounce grated cheddar cheese

Line dish with bananas, pineapple and marshmallows. Dissolve Jell-O in 1½ cup boiling water, add 1½ cups cold water and pour over items in dish. Put in refrigerate until Jell-O sets. Cook 1 cup pineapple juice, 2 tablespoon flour, and 2 tablespoons butter, until thick. Cool, then add 1 cup sour cream. Spread over top of Jell-O. Sprinkle cheddar cheese on top.

Vanilla Pudding Fruit Salad

Moe Guthrie

1 package instant pudding
1 can unsweetened pineapple chunks
1 can unsweetened fruit cocktail
4 tablespoons orange juice
1 can mandarin oranges
1 apple (peeled and cubed)
1 banana (sliced)

Drain pineapple, add juice to pudding and orange juice. Mix well. Add pineapple, fruit cocktail, oranges , apples and banana.

Pistachio Salad

Maureen Pauli

2 small packages instant pistachio pudding
2 cans crushed pineapple
2 ½ cups miniature marshmallow
18 ounces Cool Whip
1 cup chopped nuts

Blend pudding with can of pineapple, add marshmallow and nuts, fold in Cool Whip. Chill before serving.

Cranberry Salad

Leta Marsh

12 ounce package fresh cranberries
1 ½ cup sugar
1 orange
3 ounce package strawberry Jell-O

1 cup tiny marshmallow
3/4 cup walnuts
1 teaspoon lemon juice

Grind cranberries and orange (peel and all), add sugar and lemon juice - mix and chill overnight. Add 1 ½ cup boiling water to Jell-O, let set partial. Add cranberry mixture, marshmallow, chopped walnuts - let set completely. Serve on leaf lettuce.

Green Bean Casserole

Bev Brant

2 (1 pound) cans French cut green beans (drained)
3 tablespoons butter
garlic (to taste)
salt and pepper (to taste)

2 tablespoons flour
1 cup sour cream
1/4 to ½ pound soft cheese (diced)

Drain beans, place in flat 6 x 10" baking dish. Sprinkle garlic, salt and pepper over beans. In a sauce pan melt butter, stir in flour and sour cream. Add cheese, stir until melted and thick. Pour over beans, top with bread or cracker crumbs. Bake at 350° for 30 minutes.

Kay's Kold Karrots

Kay Bogart

4 pounds carrots (peeled)
3/4 cup vinegar
1 cup sugar
1 can tomato soup
2 teaspoon salt

½ cup light oil
1 tablespoon dry mustard
2 tablespoon Worcestershire
1 large green pepper(diced)
1 large onion (diced)

Cut carrots on a slant. Cook until firm. Boil sugar and vinegar, add oil, tomato soup, mustard, Worcestershire and salt. Stir. Drain carrots thoroughly and place in a container with lid. Add onions and green pepper. Pour liquid over vegetables. Marinade in refrigerator for at least 12 to 24 hours. Stir frequently. Serve at room temperature.

Gulliver's Corn

Betty Elchuck

40 ounces frozen corn
1 cup whipped cream
1 cup milk
dash white pepper
2 tablespoon sugar
1 teaspoon salt
2 tablespoons butter
2 tablespoons flour

Combine all ingredients (except butter and flour) in saucepan. Bring to a boil, reduce heat and simmer for 5 minutes. Blend together butter and flour and stir into corn until thickened.

Zucchini Casserole

Carrie Cygan

2 to 3 large zucchini (cut ½" slices)
2/3 cups sour cream
1 tablespoon butter
1 cup grated cheddar cheese
½ teaspoon seasoning salt
½ cup bread crumbs
½ cup milk

Heat oven to 375°. Cook zucchini 10 to 15 minutes in water, drain. Put in casserole dish. In saucepan combine sour cream, butter, cheese, salt and milk. Heat, stirring until blended. Pour over zucchini. Top with bread crumbs. Bake for 10 to 15 minutes, or until bread crumbs are golden.

Broccoli Casserole

Billie Bruckner

4 oounces shredded cheddar cheese
1 cup cooked long grain rice
½ cup sliced mushrooms
½ cup diced onions
½ cup skim milk
1 1/4 tablespoon margarine
20 ounces frozen broccoli
1 teaspoon salt

Preheat oven to 350°. Spray 2-quart casserole dish with non-stick cooking spray, set aside. In a 3-quart saucepan combine all ingredients except broccoli and salt and cook over medium heat, stirring constantly, until cheese and margarine are melted. Add broccoli and salt and cook stirring frequently until broccoli is heated, about 2 minutes. Turn into sprayed casserole dish and bake until mixture is heated throughout and broccoli is tender, about 30 minutes.

Onion Cheese Casserole

Moe Guthrie

2 cups finely crushed buttered flavored crackers (about 45)
½ cup butter
3 pounds onions (sliced thin)
2 tablespoons flour
½ pound pasteurized cheese (cut up)
½ teaspoon black pepper
½ teaspoon salt
2 cups milk
sweet red pepper
(cut into rings)
fresh jalapeno pepper

Preheat oven to 350°. Spread 1 cup cracker crumbs in greased 9 x 11" dish. In large skillet saute onions in 1/4 cup butter. Spoon onions over cracker crumbs. Melt remaining butter, stir in flour, salt and black pepper. Gradually stir in milk, stirring constantly. Cook until thick. Add cheese and stir until smooth. Pour cheese mixture over onions. Sprinkle remaining cup of cracker crumbs over cheese mixture. Bake 25-30 minutes. Garnish with red pepper rings and jalapeno pepper.

Sour Cream Potatoes

Chuck & Pattie Ashby

2 pounds frozen hash brown potatoes
1 pound sour cream
1 can cream of chicken soup
8 ounces shredded Jack or cheddar cheese
1 cup chopped onions
1 stick margarine (melted)
salt and pepper to taste
bread crumbs

Combine all ingredients (except margarine and bread crumbs). Put in 9 x 13" glass baking dish. Sprinkle bread crumbs over top. Pour butter over bread crumbs. Bake at 350° for 1 hour.

Cheese Potatoes

Kathleen Cygan

5 to 8 whole potatoes
1/4 cup chopped green onions
3/4 cup grated cheddar cheese
1/4 cup melted butter
1 teaspoon seasoning salt
½ cup sour cream

Cook potatoes in boiling water, with skin on. When cooled remove skins. Coarsely grate potatoes, add melted butter, sour cram, salt, green onions and cheese. Mix. Put in casserole dish. Bake at 375° for approximately 40 minutes.

Potato Casserole

Ellen Alkire

1 package Tater Tots (or hash browns)
1 can cream of mushroom soup
1 small container sour cream or cream cheese
1 can cheddar cheese soup
onion bits

Heat oven to 350° Mix soups and sour cream and pour over TaterTots. Sprinkle onion bits over top and bake for 40 minutes.

Mahoney's Potatoes

Hazel Tippings

1 bag frozen hash brown potatoes
1 can undiluted cream of chicken soup
1 medium chopped onion
2 cups shredded sharp cheddar cheese
16 ounces sour cream
2 cups crushed corn flakes
1 1/4 sticks melted butter
salt and pepper

Place frozen potatoes in bottom of 13 x 9" baking dish. Drizzle 1 stick of melted butter over potatoes. Mix in bowl soup, sour cream, onion, cheese, salt and pepper. Spread over potatoes. Mix corn flakes and 1/4 stick melted butter. Spread over cheese mixture. Bake at 350° for 1 hour. *(You can mix ahead and bake later.)*

Hilda's Creamed Spinach

Bobbi Holmes

1 box frozen chopped spinach
3 tablespoons butter
2 to 4 tablespoons flour
salt and pepper to taste

Cook spinach according to directions on package, set aside. In a saucepan melt butter and mix together flour to form paste. Add hot spinach and stir well over medium fire. Add more or less butter, flour, or salt and pepper, according to personal taste. Garnish with slices of hard boiled eggs.

Grandma Smith's Baked Beans

Debbie Loyd

3 cups navy or northern beans
2 teaspoons finely chopped onions
2 tablespoons brown sugar

3 strips bacon (lightly fried)
1/4 cup ketchup
Dab of mustard

Best to use in a bean pot - layer beans, onion, brown sugar, bacon, ketchup, mustard, until pot is half full. Cover with water until beans are covered. Add water throughout the day. Put a lid on pot and bake in 325° oven until done - usually takes all day

Minnesota Baked Beans

Dianne Ramirez

1 pound ground beef
1 can pork and beans
1 can lima beans
2 tablespoons mustard
2/3 cup ketchup

6 slices bacon
1 can kidney beans
3/4 cup brown sugar
2 tablespoons Worcestershire
onion

Brown beef and onions. Drain. Mix well with other ingredients and bake in a 9 x 13" pan at 350° for 1 hour.

Meats & Poultry 🍎

Sweet and Sour Spare Ribs
Bev Brant

1 - 3 pounds farmer style spare ribs
1½ cups brown sugar
2 cups soy sauce
16 ounces crushed pineapple
garlic powder (to taste)

Heat brown sugar, soy sauce and garlic powder until sugar is dissolved. Cool 5 minutes, add pineapple, including juice. Pour over ribs, bake at 350° 1 to 1 ½ hours, covered.

Liverwurst Roll
Dori Plathe

1 pound liverwurst
8 ounces cream cheese
3 tablespoon minced onion
½ teaspoon sweet basil dressing
½ cup chopped walnuts
1 clove garlic (minced)
1 teaspoon Tabasco sauce
1 teaspoon salad

Mix together (in order listed) liverwurst, 1/3 of the cream cheese, onion, basil and walnuts. Form into rolls (like jelly rolls) and set aside. In a separate bowl combine remaining cream cheese, garlic, Tabasco and salad dressing. Spread over rolls, roll up and then roll in chopped nuts or parsley or chives. Freeze until ready to use.

Pork Chops in Sour Cream Sauce
Mary Waters

6 loin pork chops
½ cup water
2 tablespoons brown sugar
2 tablespoons fine chopped onion
2 tablespoons ketchup
1 clove garlic (minced)
1 beef bouillon cube
2 tablespoons flour
½ cup water(for sauce)
½ cup sour cream

In large skillet brown pork chops. Add ½ cup water, brown sugar, onion, ketchup, garlic and bouillon. Cover, simmer for 30 to 40

In large skillet brown pork chops. Add ½ cup water, brown sugar, onion, ketchup, garlic and bouillon. Cover, simmer for 30 to 40 minutes or until tender. Remove chops to serving platter and keep warm. In a small bowl combine flour with 1/4 cup water, slowly add to cooking liquid stirring constantly. Cook until thickened. Stir in sour cream and heat thoroughly (do not boil). Serve over chops.

Burgundy Roast

Kay Bogart

2 tablespoons butter
1 dozen medium mushrooms
3 pounds rump roast

1 envelope Lipton's Dry Onion Soup mix
2 cups burgundy wine

Heat oven to 375°. Melt butter in a large skillet over medium heat. Add ½ cup burgundy and brown roast on all sides. The wine will be absorbed by the meat. Fold 2 long sheets of foil together lengthwise in a shallow roasting pan. Put roast in middle. Pour 1 ½ cup of wine over roast, place mushrooms on top of and around the roast. Sprinkle with onion soup - covering top and sides. Bring long edges of foil over meat and seal with a double fold, making a tent effect. Seal ends of foil. Roast about 2 ½ hours in the oven. *Juice makes excellent gravy or you can serve it au jus.*

Chinese Hamburger Chow Mein

Moe Guthrie

1 pound lean hamburger
2 tablespoons soy sauce
1 tablespoon celery flakes
1 tablespoon instant bullion
1 can cream of mushroom soup

3 ½ cups water
can chow mein vegetables (drained)
2 tablespoons cornstarch
chow mein noodles

Brown hamburger in large pan, drain off grease. Add ingredients except ½ cup water and cornstarch, mix and put aside. Stir in hamburger mixture to blend and simmer 15 minutes. Bring to a boiling point and add water and cornstarch mixture, stirring constantly as the mixture thickens. Serve over chow mein noodles.

Chicken Cordon Bleu

Julie Little

1 chicken breast (boned)
1 slice Swiss cheese
1 slice ham
1 egg (beaten)
1 ounce flour
1 ounce Contadina seasoned bread crumbs
1 ounce melted butter

Pound chicken to 1/4 inch thickness. Place cheese slice and ham on flat breast. Roll up, roll first in flour, egg and coat with bread crumbs. Place in baking dish and pour melted butter over it. Bake at 350° for 30 to 40 minutes.

Ortega Chili Chicken

Hazel Tippings

8-12 chicken breasts
16 ounces sour cream
large can chopped Ortega chiles
2 cups shredded Jack cheese
oil
garlic salt (to taste)
pepper (to taste)
salt (to taste)

Brown chicken in hot oil. Season with pepper, salt and garlic. In bowl mix sour cream, chiles and cheese. When chicken is brown place on broiler pan. Spread cheese mixture over each piece of chicken. Place in oven and broil until cheese melts and top is brown. Topping mixture should be relatively thick and spreadable.

Oma's Fried Chicken

Oma Head

chicken (cut up and clean)
flour
buttermilk
seasoning

One of my favorite Havasu originals was Oma Head - a dear spunky lady who loved to fish, was one hell of a cook, and in many ways was a grandmother to me. She and her husband Aubrey had a trailer along Whipple Bay. They eventually retired in Havasu City, and spent time both at the Palms and at Havasu City. In high school I often stayed with the Heads, so I wouldn't have to travel back across the lake at night. To say I was well fed during my visits, would be an understatement. Oma believed in homemade biscuits and pork chops and gravy for breakfast! At Christmas time she made homemade divinity

- *which was the best I ever tasted. One of her specialities was fried chicken. She shared with me her secrets for divine old fashioned fried chicken. Oma and Aubrey both passed away in the early 1990's. Yet their memory is woven into the rich history of Havasu Palms - Bobbi Holmes.*

Add flour to a bowl and season as desired. Pour buttermilk into a separate bowl. Dip each chicken piece in flour (completely covered), then dip in buttermilk (completely covered), then dip again in flour (completely covered). Fry in hot oil, turning constantly and cooking slowly. Cook until crispy - about one hour.

Chicken Parmesan

Sandy Loyd

4 chicken breasts (boneless & skinless)
1 egg (slightly beaten)
½ cup seasoned bread crumbs
2 tablespoons butter
1 3/4 cup Prego Spaghetti sauce
½ cup shredded mozzarella cheese
1 tablespoon grated Parmesan cheese
1/4 cup chopped parsley

Use palm of hand to flatten chicken to even thickness. Dip chicken into egg, then into crumbs to coat. In skillet over medium heat, brown both sides of chicken in melted butter. Add Prego sauce. Reduce heat. Cover and simmer 10 minutes. sprinkle with cheese and fresh parsley. Cover, simmer 5 minutes or until cheese melts.

Don't Peek Chicken

Gary Swint

6 chicken thighs
1 cup rice (not instant)
2 teaspoons melted butter
1 can cream of mushroom soup
1 can cream of chicken soup
½ can condensed milk
1 package Lipton's Dry Onion Soup mix

Put rice in bottom of roasting pan, add chicken, then remaining ingredients. Seal tightly with foil. Bake at 2 ½ hours at 325°.

Chicken Imperial

Mary Waters

2 cups cracker crumbs
½ cup minced parsley
1 clove garlic (minced)
1/8 teaspoon pepper
1 cup melted butter

1 tablespoon Dijon mustard
1 teaspoon Worcestershire
8 whole chicken breasts
(boned and halved)

Combine cracker crumbs, parsley, garlic and pepper. Mix together butter, mustard and Worcestershire. Dip chicken first in butter mixture then roll in crumb mixture, making sure to coat all sides. Place chicken in a shallow baking pan. Sprinkle chicken with the remaining butter mixture and bake uncovered at 350° for about 1 hour. Do not overcook.

Main Dishes & Casseroles

Our Favorite Casserole
Rich & Donna Middlebrough

1 package hash brown patties or cheddar browns
1 tube Jimmy Dean Sausage or 1 pound bacon
10 eggs (beaten)
1 diced bell pepper (optional)
1 medium onion (diced)
1 bag shredded cheese
sour cream
salsa

Layer in buttered 9 x 13" casserole dish: hash browns, cooked and crumbled sausage or bacon, diced onion and bell pepper, eggs, and top with shredded cheese. Bake at 350° for 1 hour or until eggs are set up. Top with sour cream or salsa. *For low fat options, substitute with egg beaters, low fat cheese, or low fat turkey sausage*

Whipple By Breakfast Burrito
Brent Benson

1 dozen eggs
1 pound bacon
10-12 slices real American cheese
flour tortillas
½ cup condensed milk
6-8 ounces chorizo
salt & pepper

In large skillet fry bacon to desired crispness. Remove bacon and all but 3-4 tablespoons of bacon grease. Squeeze choriso from casing into skillet and cook over medium heat, stirring until mixture is thin and bubbles. Remove from heat. Tear cheese into quarters and add to mixture. Add eggs, salt and pepper and milk. Gently stir mixture until all ingredients are combined. Do not whip! (*As this stage the mixture is extremely volatile - therefore no smoking should be permitted within 50 feet*) Return to medium heat and continue to stir slowly until mixture is firm. Eggs are ready to eat when firm, but slightly creamy. Can be enjoyed naked or fill a warm flour tortilla, add bacon and dip in a side dish of your favorite salsa. Mmm...good stuff! Serves 6-8 hungry people.

Ham and Cheese Casserole
Ellen Alkire

1 can spam or ham (cubed)
½ pound sharp cheddar cheese (grated)
20 unsalted crackers (rolled fine)
2 eggs (beaten)
2 cups milk
1 can cream of mushroom soup (heated)

Mix spam, crackers, and eggs and put in baking dish. Pour milk on top and bake for 1 hour at 350°. Top with heated soup.

Sandy's Spinach Quiche
Sandy Loyd

3 ounce packet Hidden Valley Ranch
10 ounces frozen chopped spinach
3/4 cup grated Swiss cheese
9" pie crust
3 eggs
½ cup milk

Preheat oven to 350°. Puncture bottom of crust with fork and bake for 7-9 minutes. Beat eggs, add milk and salad dressing, mix well. While crust is hot fill with spinach (thawed and squeezed dry), sprinkle cheese cover top and over with egg mixture. Bake for an additional 25-30 minutes or until the quiche is firm and the top is golden.

Quiche Lorraine
Leta Marsh

9" pie crust
3/4 teaspoon salt
1 cup shredded Swiss cheese
1/8 teaspoon cayenne pepper
12 slices bacon (cooked crisp & crumbled)
2 cups whipping cream
4 eggs
1/4 teaspoon sugar
1/3 cup minced onion

Heat oven to 425°. Sprinkle bacon, cheese and onion in crust. Beat eggs slightly, beat in remaining ingredients. Pour cream mixture into pie pan. Bake 15 minutes. Reduce temperature to 300° and bake 30 minutes longer or until knife comes out clean. Let stand 10 minutes before cutting.

Five Hour Beef Stew

Lou Van Horn

2 pounds stew meat (cubed)
6 carrots (cut in chunks)
3 potatoes (cut in chunks)
1 large diced onion
5 stalks celery (sliced)
2 ½ cups stewed tomatoes
1 tablespoon sugar
4 tablespoons tapioca
salt and pepper to taste

Place all ingredients in baking dish or large pan. Cover and bake 5 hours at 250°. *No peeking. Great for wintertime. Go hiking, etc, come home and enjoy*

Kevin's Favorite Goulash

Betty Caldwell

1 pound lean hamburger
½ teaspoon Lawry's Season
3 tablespoons chopped onion
26 ounce jar Classico Four Cheese Pasta Sauce
1 can Mexi-corn (drained)
12 ounces shell pasta (cooked)
½ teaspoon pepper

Brown hamburger with chopped onions and seasoning. Drain well, add pastas sauce and corn. Simmer 10 minutes. Add drained pasta shells to hamburger mixture. *Serve with Parmesan cheese and garlic bread.*

Pineapple Apricot Chicken

Ellen Alkire

1 small jar apricot/pineapple preserves
1 bottle Kraft Catalina Dressing
1 package Lipton Soup mix
1 package chicken breast

Mix soup mix and preserves in bowl. Pour over chicken and bake at 350° for 1 hours.

Hungarian Gypsy Chicken Papricas and Galushka

Ron Rengel

Chicken:
Chicken
3 large onions (chopped)
4 cloves garlic (minced)
1 teaspoon salt
1/4 teaspoon pepper
3 teaspoons paprika
3/4 cup oil
2 teaspoons minced parsley
½ cup flour
2 quarts water

First you steal a chicken. In oil saute onions, add chicken pieces, garlic, parsley, salt, pepper and paprika. Let brown. Add water and flour, simmer until chicken is done.

Galushka:
4 eggs
1 teaspoon salt
3 cups flour
1 cup milk
½ teaspoon baking powder

Beat eggs with salt, flour, milk and baking powder. Mix until dough is smooth. Drop spoonful size pieces in pot boiling water, cook 20 minutes. Drain and serve with above.

French Country Beef Casserole

The Meeks & Rogers

Stew:
3 pounds boneless beef chuck (cubed)
salt and freshly ground pepper
24 ounces dry white wine
2 tablespoons Dijon mustard
3 large tomatoes -peeled and seeded and chopped
3 onions (quartered)
3 garlic cloves (halved)
3 tablespoons olive oil

Bouquet garni (tie the following in cheesecloth):
5 flat leaf parsley sprigs
2 bay leaves
3 thyme sprigs
2 leak greens

Brown beef in oil in a large Dutch oven. Salt and pepper generously.

Remove beef to a plate. Pour off excess oil. Add wine and cook over moderate heat. Stir in mustard and blend. Return meat and stir in tomatoes and their liquids. Add onions, garlic and bouquet garni. Cover and bring to a boil. Reduce heat to low and simmer until meat is tender. About 3 ½ hours. Let stew cool, cover and refrigerated overnight. Next day scape off surface fat and reheat. Discard bouquet garnish and bring stew to a low boil for 10 minutes. Reduce heat, serve.

Chicken Casserole with Macaroni

Doris Plathe

2 cup cut up cooked chicken
2 cups uncooked macaroni
21 ounces cans mushroom soup
1 ½ cans chicken broth
1 small onion (chopped)

½ pound cheddar cheese
1 soup can of milk
2 ounce jar red pimentos
½ teaspoon salt

Mix all ingredients in large bowl. Pour into 9 x 13" pan. Cover and place in refrigerator overnight. The next day bake at 350° until bubbly and light brown. Add grated cheese on top before baking.

Savory Baked Chicken

Doris Castro

1 cup Miracle Whip Salad Dressing
1/4 cup lemon juice
3 pounds of cut-up chicken pieces
2 tablespoons tarragon, basil or oregano leaves (crushed)

½ teaspoon salt
sesame seeds

Combine dressing, juice and seasonings, mix well. Pour over chicken, chill several hours or overnight. Reserve dressing mixture. Place chicken, skin side up (or remove skin) in baking pan. Bake at 425° for 35 minutes, brushing occasionally with dressing mixture Sprinkle with seeds, continue baking 5 minutes or until tender. *(Variations: 2 tablespoons grated lemon rind and 2 tablespoons parsley for tarragon or 2 garlic cloves minced for tarragon.)*

Sweet and Sour Chicken

Ann Ries

12 pieces of chicken
1 large bottle French dressing
1 can cranberry sauce
1 package Lipton onion soup

Blend dressing, cranberry and soup mix. Arrange chicken in single layer in covered baking dish and marinade overnight with above mixture. Bake uncovered at 350° for 1 ½ hours, turning once. *(You can substitute Russian for French Dressing.)*

Chicken Chili Crepes

La Donna Duir

8 - 10 basic crepes

Sauce:
2 tablespoons butter
1 tablespoon chicken bouillon
2 tablespoons flour
1 cup half & half
8 ounces tomato sauce

Filling:
3 tablespoons butter
½ onion (diced)
1 clove garlic
2 whole chicken breasts
7 ounce can diced Ortega chilies
1/4 teaspoon salt
½ pound Jack cheese (grated)
1/4 pound cheddar cheese (grated)

Melt butter, add flour and stir. Add chicken base, stir. Add half & half, the tomato sauce. Cook over medium heat until thick, stirring constantly. Cut chicken in 1" pieces. Melt butter in skillet, saute onions, garlic and chicken. Cook chicken until it looses its pink color. Add salt, seasoning, chilies and ½ cup of sauce. Stir and cook over low heat for 5 - 10 minutes. Mix cheeses. Fill crepes with chicken mixture and sprinkle about 3 tablespoons of cheese mixture over chicken, roll up. Place in baking dish. Pour remaining sauce over top. Sprinkle cheese over sauce. Bake at 400° for 10 - 15 minutes.

Blue Ribbon Meat Loaf

Maureen Pauli

1 envelope dry onion soup mix
1 cup sour cream
1 ½ pounds ground beef
2 egg (slightly beaten)
1 cup bread crumbs
2 strips bacon

Combine onion soup, sour cream and eggs. Mix ground beef, add bread crumbs, mix well. Shape into loaf and lay bacon on top. Place in preheated 500° oven. Reduce heat to 375° and bake for 1 hour.

Best Meat Loaf

Kelly Barry

1 ½ pound lean ground beef
1 cup milk
1 egg (lightly beaten)
3/4 cup soft bread crumbs
1 medium onion (chopped)
1 tablespoon chopped green pepper
1 teaspoon dill weed
1 tablespoon ketchup
1 ½ teaspoon salt
1 teaspoon prepared horseradish
1 teaspoon sugar
1 teaspoon ground allspice
Addition ketchup

In a large bowl combine the first 12 ingredients. Mix well. Press into an ungreased 8 ½ x 4 ½ x 2 ½" loaf pan. Bake at 350° for 1 hour. Drizzle top of loaf with ketchup. Bake 15 minutes more or until no pink remains. Yields 6-8 servings.

Juicy-Cheesy Meat loaf

Mary Nichols

2 pounds ground beef
1/4 cup chopped green pepper
3/4 cup chopped onion
2 eggs (beaten)
1 cup diced Velveeta cheese
2 cups Italian bread crumbs
1 ½ cup V-8 Juice
2 teaspoons salt
1/4 teaspoon pepper
1 teaspoon Nature's Seasoning

Combine all ingredients. Put in 9 x 5 x 3 loaf pan. Bake for 1 ½ hour at 350°.

Tamale Pie

Shirley Rojas

1 ½ cup yellow cornmeal
2 cups milk
2 large onions (diced)
1 ½ pound ground beef
1 small can whole corn

2 pods garlic
8 ounces tomato sauce
a few black olives
chili powder to taste
salt to taste

Combine cornmeal and milk. Let sit for 4 hours. Fry onions, garlic and meat until brown. Add chili powder, tomato sauce, salt, corn, cornmeal add olives. Mix together. Put in buttered 9 x 13" baking dish and bake at 375° for 1 hour.

Cheater Chili Rellanos

Debra Oney

2 cans chilies
1 pound shredded Jack cheese
1 cup flour

2 cups milk
2 eggs

Grease pan and layer chili, then cheese, then chili then cheese. Mix flour, egg and milk and pour on top. Bake 45 minutes at 350°.

Chili Rellano Casseroles

Kelly Barry

27 ounces whole green chilies
1 pound Jack cheese
3/4 teaspoon salt
3/4 teaspoon baking powder
½ pound shredded cheddar cheese

3/4 cup flour
6 eggs
½ cup milk

Drain peppers and remove seeds if needed. Cut Jack cheese in thick strips to fit inside peppers and fill each with cheese. In a blended or with a mixer, blend eggs, flour, milk, baking powder and salt until smooth. Grease 13 x 9" pan with non-stick cooking spray. Pour a little of the egg mixture into pan, just to coat the bottom. Place chilies in rows in pan and pour remaining mixture over top. Crumble remaining cheeses on top. Bake at 350° for 45 minutes or until golden brown. Serves 6.

Walt's Favorite Chili Rellanos

Bobbi Holmes

can of whole Ortega chilies
Jack cheese

2 eggs (separated)
flour
hot oil

Cut cheese into strips - about the size of french fries, and no longer than the chilies. Slip one strip of cheese into each chili -be careful not to tear chili. Carefully coat outside of chili with flour (not too thick - it is needed to help egg batter adhere). Set aside. Beat egg whites until peaking like meringue. Separately beat yolks until creamy. Gently fold yolks into whites. Dip each chili into egg, coat and fry in medium-high oil. Gently turn until golden brown. Drain on paper towel. Serve with salsa.

Mexican Lasagne

Ellen Alkire

1 package cooked lasagne noodles
1 whole chicken (cooked & shredded)
3 cups shredded Jack cheese
1 can diced Ortega chilies
jalapeno peppers (optional)

1 can diced black olives
2 cans cream of chicken soup
small diced onion

In 9 x 12 pan alternate layers: noodles, soup, chicken, cheese, onions, olive, chilies, jalapenos - then layer again. Last layer should be cheese with a little onion. Bake at 350° for 15 - 25 minutes. *Enjoy!*

Chicken Enchilada Casserole

Will & Candace Wright

1 chicken (boiled & cut up)
1 medium jar green chili salsa
1 can cream of chicken soup
1 can cream mushroom soup

shredded Jack cheese
shredded cheddar cheese
tortillas

Mix chicken, salsa and soups. In baking dish layer: tortillas, mixture, cheese and tortillas. Top with black olives and cheeses. Bake uncovered at 400° for 30 minutes.

Easy Enchiladas

Debbie Loyd

1 dozen tortillas
2 pound ground beef or turkey
1 bunch green onions
2 large cans red chili sauce
1 pound grated cheese
1 can chopped olives
1 can sliced olives

Fry ground meat and onions together. In large baking dish pour ½ cup sauce on bottom and layer tortillas on bottom, cover with more sauce. Then add layer of meat, cheese, chopped olives and more sauce. Repeat twice more, ending with a layer of tortillas. Pour remaining sauce on top of tortillas and cover with grated cheese and sliced olives. Bake in 350° for 20 to 30 minutes

Mexican Casserole

Billie Bruckner

1 ½ pounds ground beef
1 medium onion (diced)
1 can cream styled corn
10 ½ ounce can tomatoes w/green chilies
8 ounce can enchilada sauce
8 ounces grated cheddar cheese
4 ounce can sliced ripe olives
diced green chilies
oregano
cumin
garlic powder
chili powder
6 large tortillas
1 cup grated Jack cheese

Brown beef, stirring to keep meat crumbly. Drain off fat. Combine ground beef with onion, soup, tomato, enchilada sauce, cheese, olives, green chilies, and spices to taste. Tear 3 tortillas into pieces and spread over the bottom of a 11 x 7 x 2" baking dish. Spread half the mixture over tortillas. Tear remaining tortillas and spread over meat mixture. Sprinkle with cheese. Bake at 325° for 30 minutes. Makes 8 - 10 servings.

Acapulco Delight

2 pounds ground beef
14 ounces green chili salsa
1 package taco seasoning
6 corn tortillas
2 cups cheddar cheese

Maureen Pauli
17 ounces refried beans
2 cups sour cream
1/4 cup Parmesan cheese
lettuce
tomato

Brown and drain hamburger. Stir in taco seasoning and water according to package directions. Simmer 5 - 10 minutes, Add green chili salsa. Place 2 tortillas in bottom of buttered 9 x 13 x 2" dish. Spread half of meat over tortillas. Sprinkle with half cup cheddar cheese. Top with 2 more tortillas, layer with beans, then 2/3 of sour cream. Place remaining tortillas over sour cream. Cover with remaining meat mixture and cheddar cheese. Sprinkle with Parmesan cheese. Bake at 350° for 20 -30 minutes. Serve with chopped lettuce, tomato and remaining sour cream.

Tagarina

Audrey Johnston

1 green pepper (diced)
1 large onion (diced)
1 ½ pound hamburger
8 ounces noodles (cooked)
2 cans Italian styled stewed tomatoes
1 can cream styled corn
½ cup cheese
½ cup stuffed olives (chopped)

Saute pepper and onions. Add hamburger and cook until pink is gone. Add cooked noodles, tomatoes, corn, cheese and olives, mix thoroughly. Transfer to casserole dish. Garnish with grated cheese and olives. Bake in preheated oven at 325° for 30 minutes or until casserole is bubbling hot throughout.

Spaghetti Sauce

Caroline Johnson

1 pound ground beef
1 tablespoon red wine vinegar
Lawry's Seasoning (to taste)
1 bell pepper (diced)
2 large cans whole tomatoes
2 tablespoons brown sugar
1 teaspoon Worcestershire
2 stalks celery (diced)
1 can sliced mushrooms
1 yellow onion (diced)
3 teaspoons salt
½ teaspoon ground pepper
2 small cans tomato paste
garlic (to taste)

In skillet cook together beef and onion, stir to crumble. Season with salt, pepper and Lawreys (to taste). Drain off fat. In a large electric crock pot place cooked meat and all ingredients. Stir well, Cook all day on low or half day on high.

Italian Garden Pasta with Chicken

Bea Reeg

3/4 pound boneless chicken breast (cut into strips)
1 package frozen Italian green beans
1 jar Ragu Hearty Pasta Sauce
1 medium zucchini (quartered & sliced)
1 tablespoon olive oil
pinch red pepper flakes
1 red pepper (thinly sliced)
8 ounces uncooked spaghetti
Parmesan cheese (grated)

In a large skillet, cook chicken 6 minutes in olive oil. Add pasta sauce and crushed pepper flakes. Bring to a boil, reduce heat. Cover and simmer 10 minutes, stirring occasionally. Meanwhile cook pasta per package directions, during last 3 minutes of cooking add vegetables to pasta cooking water. Drain pasta and vegetables well. Spoon chicken and sauce over pasta and vegetables. Sprinkle with Parmesan cheese

Quick and Easy Pasta & Clams

Ruth Chantry

1 can white clam sauce
2 cups uncooked pasta egg spirals
½ cup water
2 cups stir fried vegetables
1/4 cup mayonnaise
1/4 teaspoon black pepper
½ teaspoon garlic salt
1/3 cup Parmesan cheese

Combine all ingredients, except Parmesan cheese in large frying pan. Boil at medium heat for 15 minutes. Top with cheese.

Manicotti With Beef and Spinach

Nicole Nichols

8 ounce package manicotti noodles
1 pound ground beef
2 tablespoons butter
½ cup Italian bread crumbs
1 jar Ragu
½ small onion (diced)
2 eggs (lightly beaten)
1 clove garlic (crushed)
½ teaspoon basil
1 teaspoon salt
dash pepper
10 ounces frozen spinach (defrosted & squeezed dry)
grated Parmesan cheese

Cook noddles. Lift with slotted spoon and place in bowl of cold water. Saute onions and garlic in butter. Add spinach, heat until moisture is absorbed. Transfer to large bowl. Brown beef. Add to spinach mixture, bread crumbs, 1/4 cup Parmesan cheese, eggs, basil and seasoning. Blend well. Drain noodles and fill with meat mixture. Pour sauce to cover bottom of 9 x 13" baking dish. Lay manicotti side by side. Top with remaining sauce and sprinkle with Parmesan cheese. Bake uncovered at 350° for 20 minutes.

Sauerkraut Pie

Ruth Chantry

1 ½ pounds ground beef
15 oz can sauerkraut (drained)
8 cups cooked instant potatoes
1 ½ cups cheddar cheese (shredded)
salt & pepper

Saute beef, salt and pepper to taste. Drain. Place in 9 x 13" baking dish. Cover beef with sauerkraut, then layer with potatoes, then top with a layer of cheese. Bake for 35-40 minutes or until cheese melts and potatoes are lightly brown.

Sauerkraut

Margaret Mushinskie

1 large can sauerkraut
1 head cabbage (shredded)
2 chopped onions
1 can small tomatoes
6 pieces celery (chopped)
1 pound bacon
(cut in small pieces)
1 pound pork chops
or Polish sausages
(cut in small pieces)

Brown meat. Put all ingredients in large pan. Cook for about 3 hours.

Squash Pie

Sue (Kanz) Hardy

1 Pillsbury pie crust
8 - 10 medium zucchini (chopped)
1 medium onion (chopped)
6 ounces grated cheddar cheese
6 ounces grated mozzarella cheese
Nature's Seasoning Salt
1 small sliced tomato
2 tablespoons mayonnaise
Italian sausage (optional)
butter

Line pie pan with crust. Lay sliced tomato on bottom of crust. In a separate bowl add zucchini and onion, dot with butter and microwave for 10 minutes. Drain and add to pie crust. Mix cheeses with mayonnaise and mix. Top squash with cheese mixture and bake for 400° for approximately 20 - 25 minutes. Add browned sausage to mixture. Serve with salsa.

Breads 🍒

White Bread

½ cup warm water
2 packages dry yeast
1/4 cup sugar

Hilda Glandon Meredith
1/4 cup shortening
3 ½ cups potato water
10 - 11 cups flour

In a small bowl mix yeast with ½ cup warm water and let it stand for 5 minutes to dissolve. In another bowl, cream together sugar and shortening. Add remaining water, dissolved yeast and most of the flour. Mix together and let rest for 10 minutes. Add just enough of the remaining flour so that the dough is not sticky. Knead until the dough is smooth and elastic. Place dough in large buttered bowl, cover and let rise in a warm spot until double in bulk. Punch down and shape into three loaves. Place in 3 buttered loaf pans, cover and let double in bulk again. Bake for 40-45 minutes at 375°.

Pumpkin Bread

Lynn Galloway

3 cups flour
2 teaspoons baking soda
1 teaspoon salt
1 tablespoon cinnamon
1 tablespoon nutmeg

3 cups sugar
1 cup oil
4 eggs
2/3 cups water
16 ounce can pumpkin

Sift together dry ingredients. Blend oil, eggs, water and pumpkin. Blend together with dry ingredients. Blend well. Pour into three butter and floured loaf pans. Bake at 350° for 50 to 60 minutes.

Date Loaf

Leta Marsh

1 pound box dates (cut-up)
2 cups marshmallows (cut-up) crumbs

1 cup cream
4 cups graham cracker
2 cups walnuts (cut-up)

Mix cut-up dates, marshmallows and walnuts with cream and 3 ½ cups graham cracker crumbs. Form into loaf. Pat remaining ½ cup graham cracker crumbs over and around loaf. Refrigerate.

Cornbread
Kelly Barry

1 3/4 cups Bisquick
3/4 cup sugar
½ cup yellow cornmeal
1/4 cup melted margarine
2 eggs
1 cup milk

Mix all ingredients in a bowl - do not use electric mixer. Pour into an 8 x 8" greased pan and bake at 350° for 25 to 40 minutes. Recipe can be doubled and baked in a larger oblong pan.

Pauline's Corn Bread
Rich & Donna Middlebrough

1/4 pound butter (melted)
2 boxes Jiffy Brand Corn Muffin Mix
1 can creamed corn (undrained)
1 can whole corn (drained)
1 cup sour cream
2 eggs (beaten slightly)

Combine all ingredients, blend well. Pour into buttered casserole dish and bake uncover at 375° to 400° for 35 to 45 minutes.

Banana-Blueberry Bread
Penny Owens

1 cup white sugar
½ cup butter
2 eggs
3 tablespoons sour milk
1 level teaspoon baking soda
2 cups flour
dash of salt
3 ripe bananas (mashed)
1 cup blueberries

Mix together first four ingredients, add soda, salt and flour, then banana and lastly the berries. Pour into loaf pan (treated with non-stick spray) and bake for 1 hour at 350°. Take out of pan, cover with foil. Best when eaten next day.

Quick Banana Bread

Dori Plathe

3 stick of butter (room temperature)
6 eggs
3 cups sugar
9 bananas (mashed)
2/3 cup milk
3 teaspoons baking soda
6 cups flour

Mix well - in order listed. If desired add 1 ½ cups walnuts. Bake 45 to 50 minutes at 375°.

Bran Muffins

Bobbi Holmes

2 cups boiling water
6 cups all bran cereal
2 cups sugar
1 cup shortening
4 eggs
5 cups flour
5 teaspoon baking soda
1 teaspoon salt
1 quart buttermilk

Pour boiling water over bran, stir and set aside. Cream together sugar, shortening, then eggs. Blend and set aside. Stir together flour, baking soda and salt. Alternate adding flour mixture, then buttermilk to sugar mixture, blend. Stir bran mixture into batter, blend. Spoon into buttered muffin tin. Bake for 20 minutes at 400°. *Makes about 5 dozen.*

Malasadas

PJ & Bev Kramer

There are variations to this recipe, but this is one my family has used for over 50 years.

1 package dry yeast
1 teaspoon sugar
1/4 cup lukewarm water
6 eggs
6 cups of flour
½ teaspoon salt
½ cup sugar
1/4 cup butter (melted)
1 cup evaporated milk
1 cup water

Dissolve yeast and teaspoon sugar in lukewarm water. In a large bowl, beat eggs until thick. Mix flour, salt and sugar and add to eggs. Mix well. Add melted butter, evaporated milk and water. Thoroughly mix to obtain a soft, smooth dough. Cover, let rise until double in bulk.

With circular motion, following outer edge of bowl, turn dough and let rise again. Drop by teaspoon full into deep vegetable oil heated to 375°. Fry until golden brown. Dough will rise to top of oil, turn doughnut over to cook evenly. Drain on paper towel, roll in granulated sugar. *Makes approximately 5 dozen.*

Pies, Pasty & Dessert

Amazing Coconut Pie

Gary Swint

2 cup milk
3/4 cup sugar
½ cup Bisquick mix

4 eggs
1/4 cup butter
½ teaspoon vanilla
1 cup coconut

Combine milk, sugar, Bisquick, eggs, butter, vanilla in blender. Cover and blend on low for 3 minutes. Pour in greased 9" pie pan. Let stand for 5 minutes. Sprinkle with coconut and bake for 40 minutes at 350°.

Apple Crisp

Maureen Pauli

1 cup flour
1 cup sugar
1 teaspoon baking powder
1/4 teaspoon salt

1 egg
1/3 cup melted butter
cinnamon
6 - 8 tart apples

Peel, core and cut apples. Place in a buttered 9 x 13" dish. Mix flour, sugar, baking powder and salt, add unbeaten egg and work into a crumb mix. Cover apple with mixture, sprinkle top with cinnamon. Bake at 350° for 35 - 40 minutes. Serve with ice cream.

Quick Dessert

Chuck & Patti Ashby

3 cans fruit pie filling
1 yellow super moist cake mix

1 cup melted butter
1 package sliced almonds

Put pie filling on bottom of 9 x 13" pan. Sprinkle dry cake mix over pie filling. Spoon butter over dry cake mix. Add nuts on top. Bake at 350° until golden brown.

Peach Kuchen

Bea I. Reeg

1 cup flour
1 cup powdered sugar
1/4 teaspoon salt
½ cup butter
45 ounces can peaches (diced)
3 tablespoons flour
1 cup sour cream
1 small Cool Whip

Mix first four ingredients into crust and pat into 9 x 13" pan. Arrange peaches over crust. In a separate bowl mix remaining ingredients and spread over peaches. Bake at 450° for 10 minutes, reduce heat to 325° and bake for 35 minutes. Cool, top with Cool Whip.

Auntie Carie's Blueberry Cream Cheese Shortbread

Shanon & Mark Kramer

1 cup butter
4 tablespoons powdered sugar
2 cups flour
½ cup chopped walnuts
8 oz cream cheese
3/4 cup powdered sugar
1 teaspoon vanilla
8 ounces Cool Whip
1 can blueberry pie filling

Combine first four ingredients, press into 8 x 13" pan. Chill for ½ hour, then bake at 350° until lightly brown. Mix 3/4 cup sugar and cream cheese. Fold in Cool Whip and vanilla. Pour into crust, chill until served. Top with chilled blueberries before serving. *You can prepare this dessert the night before; convenient when planning a party. This is a staple desert we have at our family gatherings. It's devoured in no time!*

Cheese Torte

Donna Weinberger

2 tablespoons plain gelatin
½ cup cold water
2 eggs (separated)
½ teaspoon salt
½ cup milk
1 cup sugar
1 pound hoop cheese
(or cottage cheese)
½ teaspoon vanilla
1 pint whipping cream
graham cracker pie crust

Mix cold water and gelatine - set aside. Beat egg yolks slightly, add sugar and salt and milk. Cook in double boiler, stirring constantly, until like a custard. Add gelatine mixture to custard and beat until light and fluffy. Whip cream and beat egg whites until stiff, then fold both into custard. Pour into graham cracker crust.

Blueberry Torte

Lou Van Horn

22 graham crackers (crushed)
1 ½ cup sugar
½ cup melted butter
1 teaspoon cinnamon

8 ounces soft cream cheese
½ cup sugar
2 egg
1 teaspoon vanilla
1 can blueberry pie filling

Mix first four ingredients to form crust. Spread in 8 x 8" pan. Combine next four ingredients and spread over crust. Bake 20 minutes at 350°. Cool and top with blueberry filling. Refrigerate 8 hours before serving. Cut in bar size and top with Cool Whip. *Bon Appetit!*

Coconut Turnovers

Keene Hodges

1 bag shredded coconut
1 box ready made pie crust

1 cup sugar
1 tablespoon butter

Preheat oven to 350°. Mix coconut, butter and sugar. Cut pie crust into squares. Put a tablespoon of mix in center of each square, fold to make a triangle. Pinch edge all around to seal. Butter bottom of pan and bake until golden brown. EAT.

Grasshopper Pie

Kay Bogart

Pie Crust:
1 prepared chocolate crumb pie crust or
1 ½ cup chocolate wafers, crumbled
1/3 cup butter (softened)
3 tablespoons sugar

Use prepared crust or mix ingredients for crust. Press crumb mixture into bottom and sides of 8" pie crust (reserve a few spoonfuls for top). Chill pie crust while preparing filling.

Filling:
½ cup milk
4 tablespoons green creme de mente
2 tablespoons white creme de cocoa
24 marshmallows
1 cup heavy cream

Combine marshmallows and milk and heat until marshmallows are melted. Stir in creme de mente and cocoa. Whip cream and fold into mixture. Fill pie crust. Garnish with reserved crust crumbs and refrigerate or freeze until ready to serve.

Homemade Brownies

Will & Candace Wright

1 cup flour
2 cups sugar
4 eggs
1 cup unsweetened cocoa
2 sticks of butter
1 teaspoon vanilla.

Mix together all the ingredients. Pour in greased and floured 13 x 9" pan. Bake at 325° for 35-40 minutes. Cool and sprinkle with powdered sugar.

Grandma Smith's Rice Pudding

Debbie Loyd

1 quart milk
3/4 cup white rice
½ cup (or more) sugar
1 teaspoon vanilla
1 large egg (separated)

Put milk and rice in top of double boiler on medium heat until almost done. Take 1 egg yolk add some of the hot mixture to it then mix and put it back in mixture in double boiler. Then beat 1 egg white and pour in milk, rice and egg mixture and mix well. Add 1 teaspoon vanilla. Pour in bowl and chill. Serve with brown sugar and cinnamon on top.

Peanut Marshmallow Squares

Dianne Ramirez

Crust:
1 ½ cups flour
½ cup butter (soft)
½ teaspoon salt
2/3 cup brown sugar

½ teaspoon baking powder
1/4 teaspoon baking soda
1 teaspoon vanilla
2 egg yolks

Topping:
2/3 cup light corn syrup
1/4 cup butter
2 teaspoons vanilla
12 ounces peanut butter morsels

2 cups Rice Crispies
2 cups peanuts
3 cups marshmallow

Combine crust ingredients and press into 9 x 13" pan. Bake at 350° for 12-15 minutes or until golden brown. Place marshmallows on crust and bake for 2-3 minutes. Cool. In a separate pan combine corn syrup, butter, vanilla, and peanut butter morsels. Cook, mix together until smooth and melted. Add Rice Crispies and peanuts. Spread mixture over marshmallow. Chill before serving. *Better if made the day before.*

Layered Pudding Dessert

Chuck & Patti Ashby

1 stick butter (softened)
1 cup flour
1 cup chopped nuts
2 tablespoons sugar
1 large container Cool Whip
1 cup powdered sugar

8 ounces cream cheese
1 large package vanilla instant pudding
1 large package chocolate instant pudding
3 cups milk

Mix together butter, flour, nuts and sugar. Pat into 9 x 13" pan. Bake at 350° for 10 minutes or until lightly brown. Mix together ½ of the Cool Whip, powdered sugar and cream cheese. Pour mixture over cooled crust. Combine puddings and milk, beat until thick. Spread over cream cheese layer. Spread remainder of Cool Whip over top. Sprinkle with grated chocolate or nuts. Refrigerate.

Vanilla Ice Cream

Ordelia Loyd

5 eggs
1 ½ cups sugar
1 can Eagle Brand milk
½ gallon milk or half & half (half & half is richer)
2 tablespoons flavoring
(may use ½ lemon,
which I like best)

Beat all together and process in ice cream maker

Walt's Hot Fudge

Walt Johnson

Walt created this recipe over 45 years ago - it has been a favorite with family and friends.

½ cup milk
1 cup sugar
4 tablespoons butter
1 square unsweetened chocolate
dash salt
1/8 teaspoon vanilla

Combine all ingredients, except vanilla, over medium heat in heavy sauce pan. Stir constantly with wooden spoon, bring to a boil. Continue to stir and cook, allowing it to thicken. Bring almost to soft ball stage. Remove from heat and stir in vanilla. Allow to cool slightly before spooning over ice cream. *The longer you cook the hot fudge - the more caramel-ly it will become.*

Cakes, Cookies & Candy

Road's End Carrot Cake

Aggie Cutting

2 cups flour
2 teaspoons baking powder
1 ½ teaspoon baking soda
1 teaspoon salt
2 teaspoon cinnamon
2 cup sugar

1 ½ cups oil or apple sauce
4 eggs
2 cups chopped walnuts
2 cups grated carrots
8 ounce can crushed pineapple (drained)

Preheat oven to 350°. Butter and lightly flour 10 x 14" cake pan. Sift together flour, baking powder, baking soda, salt and cinnamon. Add sugar, oil and eggs. Mix well. Stir in remaining ingredients. Blend thoroughly. Pour into cake pan and bake for 35-40 minutes. After cake cools frost with cream cheese frosting.

Cream Cheese Frosting for Road's End Carrot Cake

½ cup butter (softened)
8 ounces cream cheese (softened)

1 teaspoon vanilla
1 pound powdered sugar

Combine butter, cream cheese and vanilla. Beat well. Gradually add sugar, continue to beat. If too thick add a little milk. Frost cooled carrot cake.

Cherry Dump Cake

Moe Guthrie

6 ounce can cherry pie filling
1 package yellow cake mix
1 cup melted butter

1 cup flaked coconut
1 cup chopped nuts
1 can crushed pineapple

Spread pie filling evenly in 9 X 13" pan. Arrange pineapple and juice over cherries. Sprinkle with dry cake mix, cover with melted butter, coconut and nuts. Bake at 350°. Can be served with whipped cream. You may substitute apple or blueberry for the cherry pie filling.

Choco-Dot Pumpkin Cake

Ordelia Loyd

2 cups flour
2 teaspoon baking powder
1 teaspoon baking soda
½ teaspoon salt
1 ½ teaspoon cinnamon
½ teaspoon allspice
½ teaspoon cloves
½ teaspoons ginger

2 cups sugar
4 eggs
1 can pumpkin (1 pound)
1 cup vegetable oil
2 cups all bran cereal
1 package (6 oz) of chocolate chips
1 cup coarsely chopped nuts

Stir together flour, baking powder, soda, salt, spices and sugar, set aside. In large bowl, beat eggs until foamy. Add pumpkin, oil and bran cereal, mix well. Add flour mixture, mixing only until combined. Stir in chocolate chips and nuts. Spread in ungreased 10 x 4 tub pan. Bake at 350° for about 1 hour and 10 minutes. If desired, drizzle with powdered sugar glaze.

Texas Sheet Cake

Shirley Rojas

Cake:
2 sticks margarine
3 tablespoon cocoa
1 cup water
2 cups flour
2 cups sugar

1 teaspoon baking soda
½ teaspoon salt
1 cup sour cream
2 eggs

Icing:
1 stick margarine
6 tablespoons milk
3 tablespoons cocoa

1 box powdered sugar
1 cup chopped nuts

Bring to boil first three ingredients for cake, set aside. Sift together next four ingredients for cake. Add sour cream and eggs to flour mixture and beat. Add hot cocoa mixture and stir. Pour into a large greased and floured cookie sheet - with a rim at least ½" deep. Bake for 20 minutes at 350°. Melt together and mix icing ingredients, spread over warm cake.

Dump Cake

Jan Miller

1 can crushed pineapple in syrup
1 can cherry pie filling
1 box yellow or white cake
2 cubes of butter
½ cup chopped nuts

Grease 9 x 13" pan. Spread pineapple in bottom, spread cherry pie filling on top of pineapple, sprinkle with cake mix on top, slice butter and put on top of cake. Top with nuts. Bake at 350° for 35-40 minutes.

Better than Sex Cake

Jackie Oldham

1 box yellow cake mix
20 ounce can crushed pineapple
3/4 cups sugar
2 (4 serving size) instant vanilla pudding
3 cups milk
8 ounce Cool Whip
3/4 cup flaked coconut

Bake cake according to box directions in 9 x 13" pan. Meanwhile, bring undrained pineapple to boil with the sugar and cook over medium heat, stirring until mixture is syrupy and thick - about 3 minutes. When cake is done, remove from oven, poke holes in it with a fork and pour pineapple on top. Cook cake completely. Mix pudding with milk, beat until thick. Spread on cake. Mix cool Whip with coconut, spread over cake. Refrigerate. Cake is better if made 24 hours ahead. *Sinfully delicious!*

Lemon Cake

Gail Gammill

Cake:
1 package lemon cake mix
1 small instant lemon Jell-O pudding
3/4 cup oil
3/4 cup water
4 eggs

Icing:
½ cup orange juice
1 ½ cup powdered sugar

Bake cake in a 13 x 9" pan at 350° for 30-450 minutes. Blend frosting. Poke hot cake full of holes with a fork and pour icing over warm cake.

Cocoa Apple Cake

Betty Caldwell

3 eggs
2 cups sugar
2 sticks margarine
½ cup water
2 ½ cups flour
½ cup chocolate chips
2 tablespoons cocoa
1 teaspoon baking soda
1 teaspoon cinnamon
1 teaspoon allspice
1 cup chopped walnuts
2 cups grated apple
1 tablespoon vanilla

Cream together until fluffy, eggs, sugar, margarine, and water. Sift together flour, cocoa, baking soda, cinnamon and allspice - add to first mixture and mix well. Fold in walnuts, apple, chocolate chips and vanilla. Mix well and spoon into greased and floured 10" loose bottom tube pan. Bake at 325° for 60 - 70 minutes. Serves 12. *This is a nice moist cake that really needs no frosting.*

Turtle cake

Dianne Ramirez

1 pound light caramels
1 cup chocolate chips
1 cup pecans
½ cup evaporated milk
3/4 cup margarine
1 box German chocolate cake mix

Melt caramels, margarine, and milk. Prepare cake mix according to directions on box. Pour ½ batter in 9 x 13" pan, bake at 350° for 15 minute. Pour caramels mixture, chocolate chips and nuts on cake. Then cover with remaining batter. Bake for another 20 minutes. Dust with powdered sugar.

Very Berry Strawberry Cake

Diana Gorrell

Cake:
1 package strawberry cake mix
1 package (3 oz) strawberry gelatin
½ box (10 oz) frozen sliced strawberries
½ cup water
4 eggs
½ cup cooking oil

Icing:
½ cup margarine
3 ½ cup powdered sugar
½ box frozen strawberries
½ teaspoon vanilla

Mix together cake mix, gelatin, eggs and water. Beat at medium speed for 2 minutes on mixer. Add strawberries (including syrup). Beat 1 minute. Add oil and beat 1 minute. Divided batter evenly into 2 greased 9" layer pans. Bake at 350° for 35 - 40 minutes. Cool about 10 minutes and remove from pans. Beat margarine until smooth, add alternately sugar and strawberries, beat until smooth. Add vanilla. If frosting is too thick, add a little milk or cream. Frost cooled cake.

Pumpkin Cake

Doris Castro

1 box yellow cake mix
1 cube butter
5 egg
1 can (29 oz) pumpkin
3/4 cup sugar
1 ½ cup milk
1 ½ cup canned cream
1/4 cup butter
½ cup or more of flour
2 tablespoons brown sugar
1 teaspoon cinnamon

Mix together cake mix, 1 block of butter, and 1 egg to form crust. With palm of hand press into greased and floured 9 x 13" cake pan. Mix together pumpkin, 4 eggs, 3/4 cup sugar, milk and canned cream. Pour into crust and bake at 325-350° for 30 minutes. Mix together 1/4 cup butter, flour, brown sugar and cinnamon. Mix to a crumb consistency. Sprinkle over cake and cook for another 30 minutes.

Rum Cake

Margaret Wilkerson

Cake:
1 yellow cake mix
1 box instant vanilla pudding
½ cup oil

½ cup water
½ cup rum
3 eggs
½ cup chopped walnuts

Icing:
1/4 cup water
1/3 cup rum

1 stick butter
dash salt

Grease and flour cake pan. Spread walnuts on bottom of cake pan. Combine remainder of cake ingredients and pour over walnuts. Bake at 325° for one hour. Boil frosting ingredients for 10 minutes. Spoon frosting over warm cake.

Peanut Butter Cookies

Kelly Berry

1 package yellow cake mix
1 cup peanut butter
small peanut butter cups (optional)

2 tablespoons water
2 eggs
½ cup oil

Mix together all ingredients (except peanut butter cup). Form into ball and place on cookie sheet. After forming into a ball you can press a peanut butter cut into the center of the dough. Flatten with fork. Bake at 350° for 10 - 12 minutes.

Traditional Sugar Cookies

Betty Caldwell

3/4 cup butter
1 cup sugar
2 eggs
1 teaspoon vanilla or lemon extract

2 ½ cups flour
1 teaspoon baking powder
1 teaspoon salt

Mix together butter, sugar, eggs, vanilla. Blend in flour, baking powder, and salt. Cover and chill at least 1 hour. Roll dough 1/8" on lightly floured board. Cut into desired shapes and place on ungreased cookie sheet. Bake 6 to 8 minutes or until light brown at 400°.

Snickerdooles Cookies

Doris Castro

1 cup shortening (part butter)
1 ½ cup sugar
2 eggs
1 teaspoon baking soda
2 teaspoons cream tartar
1/4 teaspoon salt
2 3/4 cup sifted flour

Mix shortening and sugar, add eggs. Sift together dry ingredients and add first mixture. Blend well and form into balls the size of small walnuts. Roll in mixture of 2 tablespoons sugar and 2 tablespoons cinnamon. Bake at 400° for 10 minutes or until light brown.

Coconut Oatmeal Cookies

Nicole Nichols

1 cup butter
1 cup sugar
1 cup brown sugar
1 teaspoon vanilla
2 eggs (unbeaten)
1 to 1 ½ cups flour
½ teaspoon salt
1 teaspoon baking soda
½ teaspoon baking powder
2 cups dry Quick oatmeal
1 cup crumbled cornflakes
1 cup coconut
1 cup nuts
(and or) chocolate chips

Cream butter, add white sugar gradually, brown sugar and vanilla. Add eggs, one at a time. Mix well. Mix in dry ingredients, then add remaining ingredients. (You may substitute corn flakes for Rice Crispies or Special K). Drop by spoonfuls, about 1" apart on greased cookie sheet. Bake at 350°for 12-15 minutes. Makes 3 - 3 ½ dozen.

Peanut Butter Oatmeal Cookies

Mary Waters

1 cup peanut butter
1 cup butter
1 cup sugar
1 cup brown sugar
2 eggs
1 teaspoon vanilla
2 cups dry oatmeal
1 1/4 cups flour
1 teaspoon baking powder
1 teaspoon baking soda
chocolate chips (optional)

Beat peanut butter, butter, sugar and brown sugar until creamy. Add eggs and vanilla, beat well. Add remaining ingredients and mix well. Bake at 350°for 10 -12 minutes.

Lana's Famous Chocolate Chip Cookies
Lana Kramer

1 pound butter
2 cups dark brown sugar
1 ½ cups sugar
2 tablespoons vanilla
24 ounces of chocolate chips

6 cups flour
1 ½ teaspoons salt
1 ½ teaspoons baking soda
3 eggs
2 cups nuts (optional)

Preheat oven to 350°. Cream butter and sugar, add vanilla, then eggs, beat well. Mix flour, salt and baking soda in a separate bowl, then add to butter mixture. Mix well and add chocolate chips. Drop by spoonful on ungreased cookie sheet, pat down and spread just a little. Bake for 10-12 minutes. Let cool for 5 minutes. Yields approximately 3 dozen.

Chocolate Chip Cookies
Margaret Mushinskie

4 cups flour
2 teaspoons salt
2 teaspoons baking soda
2 cups sugar

1 cup brown sugar
4 eggs
2 cups shortening
1 large bag chocolate chips
lots of nuts

Mix all ingredients. Bake at 350° for about 10 minutes. *(I made these for Walt when we came down, it makes lots.)*

Oatmeal Candy
Gary Swint

2 cups sugar
½ cup milk
3 cups oatmeal

3/4 cups peanut butter
1 stick margarine

Combine sugar, milk, melted margarine, and peanut butter. Blend well. Add oats and blend again. Put into buttered pan and let stand in refrigerator.

Mint Candy Pats

Leta Marsh

1/4 pound butter
1/4 cup cream
½ teaspoon peppermint extract
1 ½ box powdered sugar
40 or so walnut halves

Whip all ingredients, (except walnuts) then pinch into small pieces. Roll into balls, then press to flatten on wax paper. Press walnut on top. Chill in refrigerator.

Coconut Chocolate

Ordelia Loyd

2 sticks margarine (soften)
1 can Eagle Brand milk
1 teaspoon vanilla
1 pound bag semi-sweet chocolate chips
2 pounds powdered sugar
1 pound bag flaked coconut
1 cup chopped nuts
1 bar par wax

Combine all except chocolate and wax, and form into balls, chill for two hours or until firm. *(I chill before making balls and also after)*. Melt chocolate and wax in top of double boiler. Dip balls into chocolate mixture twice. Chill again.

Carmel Corn

Lynn Galloway

Popcorn
2 cups dark brown sugar
1 cup butter
½ cup light corn syrup
1 teaspoon salt
1/4 teaspoon cream tartar
1 teaspoon baking soda

Mix sugar, butter, corn syrup, salt and cream of tarter, bring to boil. Take off heat and add baking soda. Stir until consistent. Toss with popped popcorn in buttered pan. Bake at 200° for 2 hours - stir occasionally.

Fudge

Gerry Guthrie

4 ½ cups sugar
1 can evaporated milk
pinch of cream of tartar
3 cups real semi-sweet chocolate chips
1 cube butter
1 teaspoon vanilla
1 cup chopped nuts

Combine in large pan sugar, milk and cream of tartar, over medium heat, stirring constantly. Bring to a full boil. Stir constantly and boil for 8 minutes. Remove from head and add chips and butter. Stir until melted, quickly remove from heat , add nuts and vanilla. Pour into buttered pan. *Instead of chocolate chips you may use naturally flavored peanut butter chips.*

Christmas Fudge

Betty Caldwell

1 ½ sticks margarine
3 cups sugar
2/3 cups evaporated milk
12 ounces chocolate chips
7 ounces marshmallow cream
1 teaspoon vanilla

Mix margarine, sugar, and milk in large saucepan. Bring to a full boil, stir constantly, boil exactly 5 minutes over medium heat. Remove from heat. Stir in chocolate chips until melted. Add remaining ingredients. Mix well. Pour into 13 x 9" pan, cool at room temperature. Cut in squares. Makes 3 pounds.

Almond Roca by Janet Nichols

Dennis & Susan Daries

9 ounces almonds (or ½ walnuts)
1 pound butter
2 cups white sugar
1 large Hershey bar

Prepare pan (line with foil). Chop almonds. Grate chocolate. Pour half of the almonds in pan. Pour half chocolate over almonds. In heavy pan cook butter and sugar, stirring constantly. Using a candy thermometer cook until 300°. Candy will turn brown. In cold water test the candy to see if crunch. When done pour candy over chocolate add almonds. Then pour remaining almonds and chocolate over candy. Refrigerate until cool. Break and eat.

Peanut Brittle

Gerry Guthrie

1 ½ teaspoons baking soda
1 teaspoon water
1 teaspoon vanilla
1 cup water

1 ½ cups sugar
1 cup light corn syrup
3 tablespoons butter
1 pound peanuts

Butter 2 baking sheets, keep warm. Combine 1 teaspoon water, vanilla and baking soda, set aside. Combine 1 cup water and corn syrup in gallon saucepan. Cook over medium heat, stirring constantly. Immediately remove from heat, stir in soda mixture, blend throughly. Pour in baking sheets and spread 1/4" thick. Cool and break into pieces.

Peanut Brittle

Shirley Rojas

1 ½ cup unsalted peanuts
1 cup sugar
½ cup light corn syrup
1/8 teaspoon salt

1 tablespoon margarine
1 teaspoon baking soda
1 teaspoon vanilla

Combine peanuts, sugar, corn syrup and salt. Cook 9 minutes on high in microwave (until peanuts are brown and bubbling). Quickly stir in butter and vanilla. Cook 2-3 minutes longer. Add baking soda, stir quickly and pour into a greased baking sheet.

Microwave Peanut Brittle

Bev Brant

1 cup sugar
1 cup Spanish peanuts
½ cup white Karo syrup

1 tablespoon butter
1 teaspoon vanilla
1 teaspoon baking soda

Use open corning ware or glass dish. Stir with wooden spoon. Combine sugar, nuts and syrup. Cook on high 4 minutes. Stir. Cook on high 3 minutes. Stir. Add butter and vanilla. Cook on high 1 minute, stir. Cook on high 2 minutes. Add baking soda, stir and pour out onto aluminum foil. When cool, remove and break into pieces.

Miscellaneous

Swedish Pancakes

Doris Plathe

4 eggs
3 tablespoons sugar
1 quart milk
pinch of salt
1/4 cup oil

Mix in order. Will be thin and runny. Cook on hot griddle. Much like crepes.

Baked Pancakes

Gary Swint

3 eggs
½ cup plus 2 tablespoons flour
½ cup plus 2 tablespoons milk
1 teaspoon sugar
3 tablespoons butter

Sizzle butter in large frying pan. Beat in egg with whip, then add all ingredients careful not to burn. Place in oven and bake at 425° for 20 to 25 minutes. Remove, sprinkle with powdered sugar and strawberries. Serves two.

Dutch Baby

Terri Blanker

1/4 cup melted butter
3 egg
3/4 cup flour
3/4 cup milk

Melt butter in 4 quart cast iron pan. In a blender whip eggs on high for 1 minute. While blender is going add flour and milk, blend another minute. Pour mixture into pan with butter at bake for 20 minutes at 425°. Serve with lemon wedges and powdered sugar or maple syrup and butter.

A Happy Cake

Moe Guthrie

4 cups love
2 cups loyalty
3 cups forgiveness
1 cup friendship

2 tablespoons tenderness
4 quarts faith
1 barrel laughter
2 cups kindness
1 cup understanding

Take love and loyalty, mix throughly with faith. Blend with tenderness, kindness, understanding and forgiveness. Add friendship and hope and sprinkle abundantly with laughter. Bake with sunshine, serve daily with generous helping.

Teriyaki Sauce

Bill Van Horn

1 button garlic (diced)
2 ½" raw ginger root (diced)
1 ½ cups soy sauce
1 ½ cups water

1 ½ cups sugar
2 tablespoons oil
1 bunch green onions (diced)

Combine all ingredients. Place in large glass jar with airtight lid. Marinate overnight if possible. Can be used with any type of meat.

Walt's Hollandaise Sauce

Walt Johnson

6 egg yolks
1/4 cup boiling water
1 cube butter (melted)

Dash salt
3 tablespoons freshly squeezed lemon juice

Blend yolks in blender, add boiling water, then butter and salt, continue to blend. Remove from blender and cook in double boiler over boiling water. Cook until thick, stirring constantly. Add lemon juice before it thickens completely. If sauce becomes lumpy, put in blender and whip for a few seconds. *Wonderful for eggs benedict or over vegetables.*

Sweet and Sour Sauce

Margaret Wilkerson

1 package onion soup mix
3 tablespoons apricot jam
½ cup pineapple chunks
thin slices of bell pepper

Combine ingredients. Add to meat during last 20 minutes of cooking.

Turkey Stuffing

Caroline Johnson

giblets and neck from 1 turkey
1 yellow onion (diced)
4 celery stalks (diced)
½ cup butter
1 egg (beaten)
2 packages Mrs. Cubbison's Seasoned Dressing
3 cups water

Wash giblets and neck, salt and pepper. Simmer in 3 cups of water (covered) until meat falls off bone. Saute onion and celery in butter until tender. Place stuffing mix in large bowl. Add sauted vegetables to stuffing. Remove meat from bones. Place meat, giblets and water in blender and liquefy. Pour liquid over stuffing, add egg and mix well. Stuff turkey *directly* before roasting.

Spicy Rice Dish

Margaret Wilkerson

1 cup cooked rice
½ cup shredded Jack cheese
1 can diced chilies
1 cup sour cream
dash of salt

While rice is hot combine all ingredients.

Baked Rice

Bev Brant

2 1/4 cup water
1 medium onion (chopped)
½ cube butter or margarine
2 beef bullion cubes
1 cup long grain rice (uncooked)

In covered casserole dish add all ingredients in order listed. Cover. Do not stir. Bake covered at 350° for 30 minutes. Stir and bake another 15 minutes uncovered.

Riscotto Italian Rice

Gail Gammill

½ ounce can mushrooms (save juice)
1/4 cup margarine
1/3 cup chopped onions
1 clove garlic
1 cup long grain rice
1/4 teaspoon salt
10 ounce can consomme
1/4 cup Parmesan cheese
2 tablespoons chopped parsley

Drain mushrooms and reserve juice. Saute mushrooms, onion and garlic in margarine. Add rice, parley and salt. In a separate pan, combine mushroom liquid, consume and add enough water to make 2 cups. Heat to boiling and pour over rice. Cover and cook on low for 25 minutes. Topwith cheese before serving.

River Dog

Brent Benson

1 dozen large flour tortillas
1 pint salsa
2 cans "squirt" cheese
1 dozen kosher dogs or smoked sausage dogs
foil and zip lock bags

Split dogs, end to end, careful not to cut all the way through. Squirt cheese down the middle of the split. Butter tortilla with 1 or 2 squirts of cheese and place dog in tortilla. Roll up tortillas if you were making a burrito. Wrap each River Dog in foil and put the whole lot in a large zip lock bag. *Now they can be taken out on the lake and when you are laying around in Steamboat or relaxing in Topock, just throw the plastic bag up on the Bimini top or anywhere in the sun and by lunch time you will have warm river dogs to dip in your favorite salsa. MMM...good stuff. Even Ralph likes 'em.*

Banana Snacks

Elizabeth & Scott Holmes

bananas
orange juice
flaked Coconut
toothpicks

Slice bananas in 1" pieces. Dip in orange juice, then cover with coconut. Serve on plate, with each banana piece speared a with toothpick.

❦ Index of Recipes ❦

Appetizers & Beverages
Artichoke Dip	73
Beef Things	73
Cheese Ball	72
Chicken Wings	73
Cocktail Meatballs	76
Dionysus Delight	75
Fried Crepe Rolls	74
Havasu Hot Chocolate	77
Lumpia	75
Mmm on Rue	73
Oriental Style Meatballs	76
Party Pizzas	74
Punta Chivato Pina Coladas	77
Puttin on the Ritz	74
Snack Crackers	75
Snack Crackers with Garlic	75
Zucchini Fritters	72

Soups, Salads & Vegetables
Best Macaroni Salad	80
Broccoli Casserole	87
Broccoli Salad	79
Caesar Salad	81
Cheese Potatoes	88
Chinese Take Out Salad	82
Chinese Chicken Salad	82
Chinese Cabbage Salad	82
Cranberry Salad	86
Garden Salad	79
Golden Potato Soup	78
Grandma's Baked Beans	90
Green Bean Casserole	86
Gulliver's Corn	87
Hawaiian Salad	84
Hilda's Creamed Spinach	89
Hot Chicken Salad	83
Jell-O Salad	85
Joy's Cabbage Salad	81
Kay's Kold Karrots	86
Mahoney's Potatoes	89
Marinated Bean Salad	83
Minnesota Baked Beans	90
Onion Cheese Casserole	88
Pea Salad	80
Pistachio Salad	85
Potato Soup	78
Potato Casserole	89
Pretzel Salad	84
Raw Cauliflower Salad	84
Seven Layer Salad	79
Shoe String Salad	78
Sour Cream Potatoes	88
Spaghetti Salad	80
Vanilla Pudding Fruit Salad	85
Zucchini Casserole	87

Meat & Poultry
Burgundy Roast	92
Chicken Imperial	95
Chicken Cordon Bleu	93
Chicken Parmesan	94
Chinese Hamburger Chow Mein	92
Don't Peek Chicken	94
Liverwurst Roll	91
Oma's Fried Chicken	93
Ortega Chili Chicken	93
Pork Chops in Sour Cream Sauce	91
Sweet & Sour Spare Rips	91

Main Dishes & Casseroles
Acapulco Delight	106
Best Meat Loaf	102
Blue Ribbon Meat Loaf	102
Cheater Chili Rellanos	103
Chicken Chili Crepes	101
Chicken Enchilada Casserole	104
Chicken Casserole w/Macaroni	100
Chili Rellano Casseroles	103
Easy Enchiladas	105
Five Hour Beef Stew	98
French Country Beef Casserole	99
Ham & Cheese Casserole	97
Hungarian Gypsy Chicken Papricas and Galushka	99
Italian Garden Pasta w/Chicken	107
Juicy-Cheesy Meat Loaf	102

Kevin's Favorite Goulash	98
Manicotti with Beef and Spinach	108
Mexican Lasagne	104
Mexican Casserole	105
Our Favorite Casserole	96
Pineapple Apricot Chicken	98
Quiche Lorraine	97
Quick and Easy Pasta & Clams	107
Sandy's Spinach Quiche	97
Sauerkraut	109
Sauerkraut Pie	108
Savory Baked Chicken	100
Spaghetti Sauce	107
Squash Pie	109
Sweet & Sour Chicken	101
Tagarina	106
Tamale Pie	103
Walt's Favorite Chili Rellanos	104
Whipple Bay Breakfast Burrito	96

Breads

Banana-Blueberry Bread	111
Bran Muffins	112
Cornbread	111
Date Loaf	110
Malasadas	112
Pauline's Corn Bread	111
Pumpkin Bread	110
Quick Banana Bread	112
White Bread	110

Pies, Pasty & Dessert

Amazing Coconut Pie	114
Apple Crisp	114
Blueberry Cheese Shortbread	115
Blueberry Torte	116
Cheese Torte	115
Coconut Turnovers	116
Grandma Smith's Rice Puddding	117
Grasshopper Pie	116
Homemade Brownies	117
Layered Pudding Dessert	118
Peach Kuchen	115
Peanut Marshmallow Squares	118
Quick Dessert	114
Vanilla Ice Cream	119
Walt's Hot Fudge	119

Cakes, Cookies & Candy

Almond Roca	129
Better than Sex Cake	122
Carmel Corn	128
Carrot Cake Frosting	120
Cherry Dump Cake	120
Choco-Dot Pumpkin Cake	121
Chocolate Chip Cookies	127
Christmas Fudge	129
Cocoa Apple Cake	123
Coconut Chocolate	128
Coconut Oatmeal Cookies	126
Dump Cake	122
Fudge	129
Lana's Chocolate Chip Cookies	127
Lemon Cake	123
Microwave Peanut Brittle	130
Mint Candy Pats	128
Oatmeal Candy	127
Peanut Butter Oatmeal Cookies	126
Peanut Butter Cookies	125
Peanut Brittle	130
Pumpkin Cake	124
Road's End Carrot Cake	120
Rum Cake	125
Snickerdoodle Cookies	126
Texas Sheet Cake	121
Traditional Sugar Cookies	125
Turtle Cake	123
Very Berry Strawberry Cake	124

Miscellaneous

A Happy Cake	132
Bake Rice	133
Baked Pancakes	131
Banana Snacks	134
Dutch Baby	131
Hollandaise Sauce	132
Riscotto Italian Rice	134
River Dogs	134
Spicy Rice Dish	133
Swedish Pancakes	131
Sweet & Sour Sauce	133
Teriyaki Sauce	132
Turkey Stuffing	133

ORDER FORM

To order additional copies of **Where the Road Ends, Havasu Palms, Recipes and Remembrances**, complete the information below (or on a copy of this form).

Ship to: (please print)

Name _____

Address _____

City _____

State, Zip _____

Day Phone _____

_____ copies of **Where the Road Ends** @ $9.35 each $_____

Postage and handling @ $2.50 per book $_____

Arizona residents add 7% tax $_____

Total amount enclosed $_____

Make checks payable to **Robeth Publishing**
Send to: Robeth Publishing
P.O. Box 223, Lake Havasu City Arizona 86405